Perfect Phrases for Dealing with Difficult Situations at Work

Hundreds of Ready-to-Use Phrases for Coming Out on Top Even in the Toughest Office Conditions

Susan F. Benjamin

New York   Chicago   San Francisco   Lisbon
London   Madrid   Mexico City   Milan   New Delhi
San Juan   Seoul   Singapore   Sydney   Toronto

The McGraw·Hill Companies

Copyright © 2008 by Susan F. Benjamin. All rights reserved. Printed in the United States of America. Except as permitted under the United States Copyright Act of 1976, no part of this publication may be reproduced or distributed in any form or by any means, or stored in a data base or retrieval system, without the prior written permission of the publisher.

9 10 11 DIG/DIG 13 12

ISBN–13: 978–0–07–159732–6
ISBN–10:   0–07–159732–8

McGraw-Hill books are available at special quantity discounts to use as premiums and sales promotions, or for use in corporate training programs. To contact a representative please visit the Contact Us pages at www.mhprofessional.com.

This book is printed on acid-free paper.

Library of Congress Cataloging-in-Publication Data

Benjamin, Susan, 1957-
    Perfect phrases for dealing with difficult situations at work : hundreds of ready-to-use phrases for coming out on top even in the toughest office conditions / by Susan F. Benjamin.
        p. cm.
    ISBN 0–07–159732–8 (alk. paper)
1. Psychology, Industrial. 2. Business communication. 3. Interpersonal communication. 4. Organizational behavior. 5. Interpersonal relations. I. Title.
    HF5548.8.B376 2009
    650.1'3—dc22   2008008612

To Erika, wherever you are, whatever you're doing, thanks for putting up with me!

Contents

Contents

Part Three: In the Spotlight—(and Not Sure How You Got There)

Part Four: When Personal Tragedies Flare Up at Work

Contents

Part Five: In the Fire of Sabotage and Insubordination

Part Six: Pressure Cookers

Contents

Part Seven: Difficult Financial Situations

Part Eight: Relationship Quagmires

Contents

Part One

An Introduction to Difficult Situations at Work

Seven Determining Factors When Addressing Difficult Situations at Work

So how do you address a difficult situation? One where numerous personalities collide? Or the stakes are high—whether involving money or a person's reputation? Or someone, maybe *lots* of someones, may be embarrassed or worse? Or should you address the situation at all? That depends on many factors. You don't want to leap in, hoping to save the day, and then realize . . . it didn't need to be saved in the first place. Nor do you want to make things better . . . only then to realize (oh no!) you made them worse. So before you say a single word or compose that e-mail, consider these *seven determining factors*. They'll help you get the right message to the right place, for the best possible result.

1. Damage That the Difficult Situation May Have Created

Sometimes, the situation may be difficult but nothing worse than that. If you overreact, whether by apologizing or offering unnecessary compensation, you may be making yourself look bad. On the other hand, an inappropriately blasé response may cost you goodwill and worse. So before you respond, assess the situation; then make your move.

2. Personality of Those Involved

Who is involved in the situation is as relevant to the way you respond as the situation itself. If you're in a formal environment, say with stodgy senior VPs or abundantly serious academics, better not make light of the situation. But if you happen to be with a bunch of sales guys whom you regularly close the weekend with at a pub, then a joke, pat on the back, or humorous e-mail may be the best antidote for the situation.

3. Culture of the Organization

Every organization has its own protocols, culture, and rules about what is and isn't appropriate. So how you respond to the difficult situation will depend on where you are at the time. Some places are extremely hierarchical. There's a definite pecking order. Want to run to the big-guy-in-charge to discuss a drastically difficult situation with his or her employees? Don't even think of it—even if you just had lunch together the day before. Instead, you'll need to go to the person next in charge. Other culture issues: the tone you use, how you relay your message, whom you cc, and, even, whether the behavior that led to the difficult situation was tolerated in that environment. If you're on your own home turf, the situation is easier than if you're on someone else's, of course. But either way, give it thought.

4. Appropriate Timing of Your Response

When you respond can be as important as how you respond. Have an embarrassing situation, like you gave inaccurate information in a report? Waiting for people to slowly discover it or allowing them to act on bad information can be disastrous. So, yes, address that situation *immediately*. But what if the situation involves a disagreeable interaction with a colleague? Maybe it will blow over. Or maybe the strong feelings will die back in time and become easier for you to address. Oh, and be careful to check your gut response; it may not be the right one. Are you an impatient type of person? You may ache to leap in, resolve the matter, and move forward. Are you an introvert?

You may want to mull it over before taking steps. Don't rely on your personal style to dictate your response; you may only be satisfying yourself.

5. Vehicle for Your Message

Should you discuss the problem in a one-on-one? Send an e-mail? What if lots of people witnessed the situation? The vehicle you choose will be pivotal to whether your response is effective. For example, if you send an e-mail during a crisis, some people may not open it. Or given the circumstances, they may be overly sensitive and react the wrong way. Besides, in putting an apology, admission, or explanation in writing, you're essentially creating a paper trail that could support or undermine you, depending. Say something in person? Then your audience may forget what you said the moment you walk out the room. Of course, e-mails or one-on-one conversations also have their bright sides. You need to determine which one, or combination of vehicles, will make you shine and not fall further into the shadows.

6. Tone That's Appropriate for You

Up until now, we've discussed what other people expect and what the culture allows. But also consider your own style. Are you a fun-loving person? Quick with a joke? Then making light of the situation can help. Of course, you may opt to temper your style; when all goes wrong, seriousness may be in order. No problem, but beware. You may inadvertently adopt an unlikely communications style, thinking that is best. Big mistake! People expect you to be you—and that's the best way to be. *Exception:* When legal issues may come into play. Then a witty retort or poorly timed response may send you to court.

7. Outcome You Want

This is last and most *definitely* not least: what you want the recipient of your message to think, feel, and, above all, do. In some cases, you just want to restore goodwill. In other cases, you might want to get him or her to take a next step: purchase a product, resist spreading gossip, or settle a problem out of court. So be strategic, and before you race to use these perfect phrases—or any others—drum up a strategy that brings results.

Part Two

Embarrassing Situations at Work

et's face it—everyone gets into embarrassing situations at work. And most usually, these are personal situations that flare up in a professional setting. Your fly is unzipped as you're giving a presentation. You e-mail a close friend about that lousy guy you're dating, and it gets broadcast to your entire internal mailing list. You have a fiery conversation about someone who drives you nuts, and that person is right outside the door. The list is endless.

Sadly, no universities offer courses on how to deal with embarrassing situations like these. Even your parents, for all their lessons and rules, didn't have much to say on the subject. So what to do? Use the perfect phrases that follow in this section of the book. They cover every situation you can imagine—and never wanted to! Of course, the nature of the embarrassing situation will be pivotal here.

- *Pretend it never happened.* This response is always helpful when the damage is minimal. Responding in any way, through a joke, an in-person apology, or a quick e-mail, may only cause people to remember something you wished they forgot. For example, Pat, a senior vice president of a technology firm, was giving a pep talk to his employees. In the middle of his talk, he emitted (and I'm embarrassed to say it) gas. Look, these things happen, right?

    In this type of embarrassing situation, Pat could adopt the "pretend it never happened" approach. And who would really care? Difficult situation over.

■ *Address the situation straight on.* If the embarrassing situation can diminish your credibility and reflect badly on you to your superiors, you must address it straight on. Soberly. Professionally. And immediately. Pat's situation was in no way egregious. But if a colleague overheard you commenting negatively on a client or ranting about a top-tier project, better take the most serious and direct route and ask for a meeting to discuss.

■ *Send a heartfelt apology.* Personally, in the case of a colleague overhearing, I think this is the least desirable choice. I find the touchy-feely route more embarrassing than the situation that inspired it. If you ask me, workplace communications should remain just that—about actions, not emotions. But if that conversation your colleague overheard was about him or her—and could cause seriously hurt feelings—a simple apology won't be enough. Make it real. Specific. And hurry.

■ *Make a joke.* This is the perfect way to diffuse a troubling bout of embarrassment. But only with the right audience. If Pat's team was composed of the humorous types (and they were), then they'd tease him eventually to his face or else joke about it behind his back. So Pat's way of handling it? He stopped, mid-sentence, and looked at the ceiling wonderingly. "Anyone heard a goose?" he asked. Everyone in the meeting laughed, and he went on with his ever-more energetic talk.

Here are more perfect phrases for situations you—or a dozen people you know—will confront at work.

A Personal E-Mail Reaches Someone Else

So maybe you're e-mailing a note to your babysitter and accidentally click on the wrong address. Not a problem. But if that e-mail is to your wife about your recent stomach problems, or worse, about your recent marriage strains, that's different. The plot thickens if it contains highly detailed information. Your best strategy is this: determine your relationship with the person who received it and the effect it might have on work. If it *will* affect your work life, you *must* address it. If doesn't . . . maybe not.

The Situation Contains Seriously Personal Information

You want a quick response from the person—to respect you and your privacy and keep the message under wraps. Start with a quick apology, and then ask for discretion.

- Sorry for sending you an e-mail intended for my _____. As you can see, things have been difficult, and I would really appreciate your keeping this to yourself.
- I just realized I accidentally cc'd you on my personal message—sorry. I would appreciate your helping me keep this difficult situation private.
- I apologize for sending you the e-mail intended for ____, and I appreciate your letting me know about it. Please keep the contents to yourself—I'm sure you understand why.
- Tom just told me that I accidentally sent you an e-mail I intended for ____. Sorry about the intrusion—as you can imagine it was for ____'s eyes only.

- I just realized I sent you an e-mail that I intended for ____. Sorry—your address was just above his in my address book, and I clicked on yours by mistake. This message is painful and private; would you mind deleting it, unopened?

The Situation Contains Mundane Information

You can take a lighter tone with this one—basically, you're trying to dissolve any ill will, no matter how slight, for cluttering up the person's mailbox. Add humor if you think your audience will respond to it.

- Sorry about sending that e-mail intended for my kid's babysitter. Now that I think of it—how about filling in if she can't make it (ha-ha)?
- Oops! Sorry to clutter up your mailbox. Didn't mean to send that last e-mail to you.
- Oh no_____ told me I accidentally cc'd you on an e-mail. Sorry about that!
- Just learned about one of the many technology glitches to hit the workplace. This time, the fault is all mine. So sorry to have accidentally sent the e-mail to my kid's babysitter your way.

The Situation Incriminates Someone Else

Whatever you do, do *not* justify or explain why you sent the e-mail. Just make sure that the person understands that the message is *not* to be repeated and that you plan to resolve whatever difficulty you're in—and the person shouldn't try. This is especially significant if you're discussing a personal view about a professional situation.

- _____ just told me that you received my e-mail about Francis. Please don't let Francis, or anyone else, know—okay? I'll discuss the matter privately with Francis soon.
- I just realized I sent you an e-mail intended for Eddy. Please disregard it—it's about a problem which I plan to resolve immediately.
- If you happened to get an e-mail from me with the subject line "_____," please disregard it. I intended to send it to Eddy for his feedback before I moved forward.
- I just realized I accidentally sent you an e-mail intended for someone else. Please pay no attention—I was just venting.

Your Boss or Senior Official Accidentally Received the Message

Not only are you embarrassed, but you jeopardized your chances of being seen as a good employee. Good employees, after all, don't waste company time on personal messages. So you need to acknowledge the situation *first*, then explain it's a rare occurrence, and, finally, apologize for it.

- I just realized I accidentally cc'd you on an e-mail to ____. Please know that I rarely take work time for personal messages, but this situation was timely and I had little choice. Sorry that it happened.
- In reviewing my e-mails, I realized I accidentally sent you one intended for ____. I don't usually send personal messages at work unless they're necessary. I hope you understand, and I am sorry for the trouble.

- I learned that you mistakenly received my e-mail about _____. If you would like to discuss it with me, please let me know—I usually restrict my personal e-mails to my computer at home.
- You probably noticed my e-mail with the very unprofessional subject line "_____." I accidentally sent it your way. If the situation wasn't pressing, I would have waited until I got home to send it. Sorry, and please know that I spend the overwhelming majority of my work hours on professional matters.

Quick tip: Okay, you know that you shouldn't send personal messages from work. But face it: you spend most of your time at work, and now and then you can't help yourself. But remember: keep the messages as professional sounding as possible. Only state necessary information, and avoid discussing troubling or volatile thoughts and feelings. Here's an example:

> *Don't*: At this point I think you're the biggest jerk I ever met. How *dare* you behave like that to me? Don't call. Don't e-mail. Get lost.
>
> *Do*: Your behavior was unacceptable—I do not want further contact.

A Personal E-Mail Reaches Almost Everyone Else

A friend, who worked for a sensitive government agency, was madly in love with a man from a country with sensitive relations with the United States. After a relationship that was far stormier than the two nations' diplomatic relations, the pair broke up and he remarried. All was well until my friend realized she was at wits' end. She loved the guy. Craved him. So in a very undiplomatic gesture, she sent along an effusive love letter that just oozed with yearning. Little did *she* know, in his country everyone has access to everyone else's e-mails, and her private message was viewed by all in his company.

How you respond depends on the culture of the work-place, the severity (or embarrassment potential) of your message, and whether you incriminated the other person. Most likely, the message will go out to your cc list. And, most likely, other people will send it around. So *someone* will probably need to address it. In my friend's case, she didn't need to respond. Her ex-love interest did it for her, saying something like this: "Just to let you know—you shared your feelings with me and the entire workplace. I am happily married, but I, and everyone else here, wish you the best of luck."

Perfect Phrases When You're the Sender of the Message

The Message Reflects Poorly on the Intended Recipient

Start by apologizing for accidentally sending the e-mail. Then say whichever one of the following applies most:

- The message did not in any way reflect _____'s opinion. I have to apologize to him as well.
- Please know that the content reflects my point of view only.

- I alone am responsible for those opinions, and they do not reflect ___'s point of view.
- I expressed that point of view on impulse; it does not fully reflect my point of view or _____'s, in any way.

The Message Reflects Poorly on a Third Party

Once again, apologize first. Then say whichever one of the following applies most:

- The views were quite out of context and should not reflect poorly on anyone—especially _____.
- The viewpoints were entirely my own, and certainly others do not share it.
- If you have read the e-mail, please understand that the perspective is entirely my own and pertains to one circumstance only.
- Obviously, if you have any questions that resulted from this e-mail, you should probably clarify it with _____.

The Message Reflects Poorly on the Recipient's Workplace (Ouch!)

Apologize, and then put the message in context—immediately. And humbly. Especially if the recipient's job or some other aspect of work will be affected.

- As you know, I am not closely familiar with your workplace, so my opinions were inappropriate.
- _____ did not in any way influence my views of your office. You should ask her about her opinions—do not rely on my insights in any way.

16

- I did not mean to insult any of you—the feelings I expressed were out of context and entirely my own.

> *Quick tip:* In this situation, you may want to invite the recipients to speak with you directly if they like.

Perfect Phrases When You're the Receiver of the Message

You can apply the phrases we discussed if you were sending the message and apply any of these strategies.

Humor

- Oops—none of you were suppose to see that e-mail. Sorry about that.
- For your eyes only, guys. So no telling, please.
- Just thought I'd share a personal message with all of my 100 closest personal friends (who happen to be on my cc list). My apologies.
- Pretend you never read this message. What message?

A Direct Approach

- Sorry about that message. ___ meant it for my eyes only.
- As you know, my situation is quite different from what ____ expresses. Sorry to catch you in the web.
- As you know, the e-mail was personal—sorry to open doors that should be closed at work!

You Send a Client a Proposal with a Different Client's Name in It

There are two things everyone in a business setting knows about proposals: (1) No one writes them from scratch. In fact, if people did, they'd never get any work done—or send more than two or three proposals a quarter. (2) Everyone acts as if his or her proposal were fresh, targeting that one, single, most remarkably valuable potential client. So if you accidentally put someone else's name in the "_____" slot, you're basically revealing a deep, dark secret . . . that everyone knows. Mostly, the mistake is embarrassing. And like most minor mistakes, it could cost you the potential client's goodwill. Of course, with the right message, it could also open doors to how great you are. Just rely on these perfect phrases.

Start by Acknowledging the Problem, So You Can Control How the Client Responds

- We just noticed we accidentally put a different company's name in your proposal.

- Oops—by mistake, we put someone else's name in the proposal.

- Our associate _____, whom you have been talking to about the project, just alerted us to the fact that another company's name is in the spot where yours belongs.

- Just wanted to let you know—somehow, _____'s name got into the proposal we wrote for you.

When You Think It's Appropriate, Apologize

- So sorry—I am really embarrassed about that mistake.
- I apologize—I don't know how that could have happened.
- Thanks for letting me know about the mistake. I feel pretty foolish!
- I'm so embarrassed about that mistake. Thanks for letting me know.
- Wow—what a mistake! My apologies.

When the Proposal Was Really Specific to Your Client

- We had an intern review the final cut—after our team developed it for you. Since we recently wrote a similar proposal, she probably got confused. Our apologies.
- As you probably know, we do cut and paste certain paragraphs discussing core services—but we designed the bulk of our proposal specifically for you.
- Somehow, one of our templates appeared in your proposal. Sorry about that.
- We borrowed information from a similar proposal. Somehow, the client's name ended up in the text.

When the Proposal Was Unique but the Name Was Not

Point out how the client's proposal was special, especially if you're providing more of something for the same price. Be specific about where this information resides.

- As you'll see on page 8 in our cost breakdown, we still provided 10 percent off all services.
- We will provide the additional services, at no additional expense, as we discussed. (See page 3, paragraph 4.)

- Because of our long relationship, we are giving you the Level 2 plan, without additional costs, as you can see in the "Details" section of the proposal.
- If you need more time to complete the project, we will be flexible. Normally, as you know, we add 10 percent to our fees, but in your case, we won't. You can find more specifics by contacting me or by looking at the cost breakdown in the last section of the proposal.

Quick tip: Most people flip through proposals quickly, looking for specific types of content— frequently cost. Then they move on. So it's possible that your reader may not read or otherwise notice the error. If so, then don't point it out. Just ignore the mistake and hope for the best. If the client *does* notice, then use the perfect phrases we just discussed.

Perfect Phrases for When You Notice the Mistake during a Presentation

Your response will depend on the audience. When possible, make a joke:

- Wow—look at that! When did you guys change your name?
- Hmmmm . . . are you really (*other client's name here*)? I know a company that has that name, too.

- How did that happen?
- Sorry about that . . . Embarrassed? Who's embarrassed?

Or address it with professional seriousness, as you would in an e-mail.

Here are two more examples:

- Pardon that mistake—we draft all our proposals for individual clients but occasionally lift a paragraph or two.
- That's the wrong name there—sorry.

Regardless, point the client to an advantage he or she alone has. Make sure that you point out the pertinent paragraph or line—this will ensure that the client remembers it and feels there is an advantage or special benefit:

- Just to remind you—if you look at page 3, we included all the provisions we discussed for your specific project.
- Bear with me for a moment, and turn to page 6. You can see I gave you all the discounts we discussed—I didn't want any of you to think this proposal was entirely canned.

Your Boss Overhears You Criticizing Something or Someone at Work

Oh boy. This is *not* what you wanted the boss to hear. But there you are, making a really bad impression on the person you least want to offend. So you better address the situation as soon as you can. Here are some phrases that will help when . . .

You Want to Introduce the Subject

- I think you may have overheard something I said, and I'd like to clear it up.
- I was wondering if we could talk for a minute about something I said yesterday.
- You may have heard me saying something rather stupid; can we talk about it?
- Do you have five minutes to address a problem I'm having? I know you heard me discuss it with ___ yesterday.
- I have had some concerns—I probably should have come to you directly, though. Do you have an opening in your schedule when we can talk?

You Want to Explain Your Comments

- Just so you know—I tend to vent now and then. So that conversation I was having yesterday with ___ was just my blowing off steam.
- I've been frustrated for some time and needed to talk it through.

- I wanted _____'s input about the best way to deal with the project. So I was discussing the problems—not all the things that are going right.
- My comments may have seemed highly critical, but in the final analysis, I think everything will work out quite well.
- I didn't think the issue was important enough to bring to you, but I did need to discuss it with someone at work.

You Were Speaking About a Specific Project

- I've worked on projects like this before and know it will turn out right. But first, I needed to address a few matters that are interfering with our progress.
- This project has had a unique set of circumstances, and it's been a challenge. To be sure, I am focused on doing it right.
- I know what it takes to get this project to be successful. But I needed input about the mistakes that continue to flare up.
- When I started this project, I hadn't anticipated these shortcomings. So I'm trying to find a way to address them.
- These problems are serious, but I'm still optimistic about the project.

You Were Speaking About a Fellow Employee

- I think ___ and I have personality issues. Since I have a hard time talking to her directly, I vent to other people.
- Even though I think that ___ and I have a difficult relationship, we can still work together productively.
- I understand that I'm not his manager, and I didn't feel comfortable bringing these issues to him directly. That's why I was discussing them with _____.

- I want you to know that _____ likes _____. That's why I went to _____ with my frustrations. I knew she would be fair.
- Overall, I've had a good working relationship with _____. But from time to time, he really drives me crazy.

You Were (Yikes!) Speaking About Your Boss

- I realize that I should have brought these issues to you directly.
- I really enjoy working here and was complaining because I want to get clarity and feedback.
- I wasn't comfortable addressing these issues with you—although that probably would have been a better choice.
- I don't think these matters really amount to much—I just needed to get them off my chest.
- Please don't think I regularly complain like that—this one issue has been on my mind.

You Were Criticizing Someone, Then Realized the Person May Have Heard

Maybe you were talking and realized that person was right outside the door. Or maybe you thought you hung up the phone or that, during a conference call, the other person was long gone. Then guess what? There the person was . . . hanging on and on. It makes you want to shrink down to the size of a soda cracker. But wait—was the person really listening? Did he or she vanish without hanging up? Do you dare raise this embarrassing subject with the person? Or do you dare *not*? These perfect phrases will help you get through this king-size embarrassment.

When You're Not Sure Whether the Person Overheard

Obviously, keep your eyes open. If the subject of your discussion seems perfectly normal, don't worry about it. Your comments may have dissolved in the air. If that person ignores you or won't look you in the eye, take hold of the situation with the perfect phrases here. And act quickly—you don't want the ill will to fester.

- Is there anything you want to discuss with me?
- Do you have any concerns we should discuss?
- Are you doing okay? (*Yes, something that simple can be a great opener.*)
- Do you have any thoughts about our talk yesterday?
- Can I help you with anything?

When You Know the Person Overheard and You Want to Open Up the Discussion

- I'd really like to discuss what we were saying yesterday.

- I'm sure our comments were hurtful, but don't take them seriously.
- Let me know if you want to discuss what we were saying—we didn't mean anything by it.
- Sorry about what we were saying—you understand we were venting at the moment.
- We were tired from all the pressure and took it out on you. Sorry.
- You know how things can get out of hand, right? This was one of those times. Sorry.

When Your Comments Were Catty but Not Related to Work

Apologize. Not because you have to—but because you mean it. Insulting personal comments are nothing but destructive at work.

- So sorry about what we said—it was out of order.
- I feel bad about what we said. We didn't mean it.
- We never should have spoken about you that way. We were being jerks.
- I apologize for what we said. We were out of line.
- I feel embarrassed about what we said earlier. Please accept my apologies. It was wrong.

When Your Comments Were Related to the Person's Performance on the Job

When You Mean It

- I'm sorry you had to hear my thoughts this way. I think we should probably discuss them.

- I probably need to discuss these issues with the boss, instead of other employees.
- Sorry you had to hear about my perspective this way, but I really do think you need to look at some issues.

When You Don't Mean It

- Sorry—I was venting and took it out on you.
- This project has been making me crazy—it really isn't about you.
- After I left, I immediately regretted what I said.
- I don't feel that way—please don't take it for anything but venting.

Quick tip: It's useless to say that you shouldn't discuss other people at work. Of course you will. Everyone does. That's how you work out issues, get helpful insights, and let off the proverbial steam. But keep these two tips in mind: (1) There's work talk, and there's meanness. Don't be mean by making fun of a person's looks, mannerisms, or spouse. (2) Be discreet. Only tell people who will keep their mouths clamped shut and give you helpful and professional feedback. And . . . make sure you're having the discussion in private. This means not in the cafeteria where the wrong ears can overhear you, and not while standing around the water fountain—real or metaphorical. Find a quiet place at a discreet time and speak *softly*.

You Hear a Coworker Criticizing You

This situation is worse than embarrassing—it hurts. So you need to think carefully about why you want to approach the person you overheard. Do you want to explain your side of the story? Get more precise information about what your coworker said? Or perhaps you want to tell your coworker to stop chatting about you and put his or her energies to better use. The perfect phrases you'll find ahead will address each of these possibilities.

But before you apply them, ask yourself these additional questions: How does the conversation affect my work life? You don't want to overreact, nor do you want to miss an opportunity to glean helpful (albeit difficult) information about yourself. Also, what is the best venue for addressing the situation? If an e-mail—beware. These don't go away. If your response is too severe, it could be used against you. Finally, which of the participants in the conversation should you approach? The one most likely to be your ally? The leader of the gang?

Once you have a clear strategy, use these perfect phrases to get results when you want to . . .

Explain Your Side of the Story

Start by making your intentions clear, and then engage your coworker in a conversation. Make sure that you don't sound overly defensive—a hard thing to do when you're inwardly fuming. Be specific about what you overheard, when appropriate.

- I overheard you and _____ discussing your views on my contribution to the project. I'd like to explain why I took the approach I did so you're clear about my motivations and what I believe will be the outcome.

- I understand that you have some reservations about my contributions to the _____. I'd like to discuss this issue with you so you're clear about my direction.
- Since you and I work together every day, I think we should discuss my work style so you have a better sense of what to expect from me and why. I am aware that you have some reservations.
- I think we need to talk about my contributions to the _____ so far. You may not be aware of my motivations, and I want to be sure we're able to work together as productively as possible.

Quick tip: Steer clear of strong language that could alienate the person you're speaking to or create an even more adversarial relationship. Remember, you're trying to put an end to the situation, not fuel it.

Do Not

- What you're doing is spreading lies, and you better shut up about it.
- You've been saying some really rude things about me.

Do

- I understand you have reservations . . .
- I want to get clarity and put an end to any discord.

Sending an e-mail? Rude or overly emotional language could be construed as harassment and will work against you.

Get Precise Information About What Was Said

Try giving the other person an opportunity to discuss the issue with you—this may or may not work. But remember, you can't force that person.

- When you were in that meeting with ____, I overheard my name mentioned. Do you have something you'd like to discuss with me?
- I heard you speaking with ____, and your tone didn't seem too happy. I'd like to know more about what you're thinking so we can settle any differences that may be hovering.
- I realized that you and ____ may be harboring some resentment. I'd like to know what the problem is so we can address it.
- If you have any problems with me, I'd like to hear them directly. Otherwise, they won't get any better.
- Since we work together every day, we should discuss differences directly. I overheard you and ___ talking. It would be helpful for you to tell me what you think.

Get a Coworker to Stop Talking

If you overheard a coworker saying rude, inappropriate, or otherwise disparaging comments, it's best to send an e-mail. That way you have a paper trail. If you opt to speak directly, send a follow-up e-mail covering what you said. Regardless, be specific when possible, including dates and individual comments. If someone alerted you to these comments, mention this in your e-mail, as well. The following perfect phrases will serve as great talk stoppers:

- I overheard you and _____ talking about me in the cafeteria yesterday. At that time, you said that I was _____ and _____. While I did not wait to hear the remainder of the conversation, I want to remind you that these comments are personal and mean-spirited and inappropriate at work.
- Several people have alerted me to the fact that you've been making disparaging remarks about my _____ and _____. This is inappropriate for the workplace and diminishes my reputation. If you have grievances about my professional performance, please tell me directly. If you have issues about me personally, please keep them to yourself.
- Several times this week, you have been making jokes at my expense, most notably at the _____ and _____. This is counterproductive and divisive. You need to stop this at once.

You *Demand* Payment from a Client Who, It Turns Out, Paid You Already

If you own a small business and are consumed with cash flow issues, this embarrassment is probably far more common than you want to admit. Of course, even if you work for a *large* business, cash flow issues reign supreme. You bill and bill and bill and wait and wait . . . and get promises that the check . . . is . . . almost . . . in . . . the . . . mail. Finally, frustrated, you send an angry e-mail. But face it, the client deserves it, right? Only to realize that envelope tucked in your box has the client's return address and contains a check. Or even worse, your bookkeeper deposited the check a week before but neglected to tell you. Try one of the following.

When the Payment Just Arrived

If the check is really late, thank the client without letting him or her off the hook:

- We just received the payment I discussed in my e-mail and have noted this in our records.

- Fortunately, the payment arrived shortly after I sent you the e-mail. We will deposit it immediately.

- The payment arrived in our office shortly after my e-mail stating it was three weeks late.

- Our office received your payment for services we provided on June 5. As you know, you still have outstanding bills for June 10 and June 15.

When the Payment Arrived a Week or Two Before

In this case, you can apologize. True the client was late—but not as late as you thought. On the other hand, a polite thank you can help smooth any residue ridges and create a faster cash flow in the future:

- Our bookkeeper just informed us that we received the check on June 1. Thank you for sending it.
- According to our records, we actually received the payment we e-mailed you about earlier two weeks ago. We apologize for our alarming message.
- After sending you the e-mail about our overdue payment, we discovered that you sent it on May 19. Thank you for your attention, and we apologize for any disturbance our previous messages may have caused.
- We received the payment—due date May 19—on June 1. So your account is settled. We apologize for our most recent e-mails.

When the Billing System Was Wrong and You Never Provided the Service

Apologize? Definitely. And be quick (and humble) about it:

- I just noted a mistake in our billing system. We have been billing you for a service we didn't provide. I am so sorry about the mistake and any confusion that caused on your end.
- Please accept our apologies. In reviewing our accounts, we realized that we have billed you for a service we didn't provide. We have corrected this error in our system and apologize again.

If Possible, Make a Joke About It

- We just discovered we never provided the service listed on our invoice B–202. Well, that explains why you never paid us! Please accept our apologies.

- Oops—we just recognized a glitch in our billing. We were hounding you for a payment you don't owe. So sorry! Please forgive the disturbance. Of course, if you want to send us the money anyway . . .

You Emphasize a Point—Strongly and in Front of Lots of People—Then Immediately Discover You're Wrong

This situation offers several layers of embarrassment. The least embarrassing is when you make a mistake in a meeting of colleagues and (we hope) friends, and someone immediately corrects you. Worse is when you are speaking as an authority at a meeting and someone contradicts your wisdom—and you realize the person is correct. Even worse, and the *most* embarrassing, is when you're giving a talk in an ultra-packed room. During the Q&A's, one of the participants corrects you about a point you mentioned earlier. Several others in the room (audibly) agree with the participant. Now what? If you're lucky, you'll have these perfect phrases handy.

When Someone Corrects You in a Small-Group Setting—Whether a Chat Room, a Series of Cc'd E-Mails, or a Face-to-Face Meeting

Say thank you, and see if the person can provide information that will help you in the future. This will help you regain control and prove that you are the ultimate professional.

- Thanks for that correction. Do you know where I can go to learn more?
- That's helpful, actually. Who is your source for this?
- Thanks for pointing that out. That changes things.
- This will help me clarify my position as we move on.
- I didn't realize that. Thanks for letting me know.

When Someone Corrects You When You're an Authority

Regain control by agreeing with the correction whole-heartedly. Appreciatively. And above all, sincerely. Then keep the conversation (or chat room comments, blogs, or e-mails) flowing.

- You're absolutely right. Thank you for that correction.
- Now that you mention it, yes, you're quite right. I appreciate your input. Now let's move to the next point.
- Good insight. Let's see how that affects the next point.
- Thanks for correcting me on that point. Now let's discuss . . .
- In his comments on my blog, ____ correctly pointed out that . . .
- ____'s point, as published in your journal, that ___ should have been ___, was correct. I appreciate that feedback. However, the conclusion remains the same, for these reasons . . .

Among Colleagues

If you have a close working relationship, and go to each other's weddings and Fourth of July parties, then you can take a distinctly personal approach. Where appropriate, add a touch of humor to dilute any tension.

- Sorry guys—he's right.
- Wow—You're right. Why didn't I know that.
- Actually, ___ is right again. So let's move on.
- Good point. Really good point. *(Simple is fine.)*

Among Clients

Try to accept the correction *without* losing your credibility by highlighting the legitimacy of your point or the ultimate value of your contribution:

- I appreciate the insights ___ provided in his e-mail earlier today. Please know that the change does not affect our outcome.
- ___ rightfully pointed out that ____. Fortunately, this means you actually get more of the _____ we provide.
- While ___ certainly raises an important point, most professionals agree that my original figure is also applicable.
- I have inputted the changes ___ made in our analysis and am sending along the revision.

You Provide Facts or Advice in a Report That Proves to Be Wrong

What a misery. You write a report. You give it to the client, your team, or your boss. This is a definitive statement of what needs to happen next, and the outcome depends on your opinions. All is well until your prediction, facts, or who knows what else turns out to be false. Embarrassing? No kidding. So start by acknowledging the mistake and, where appropriate, thanking the person for telling you about it, using these perfect phrases:

- Sorry about the inaccuracy in that report.
- Thank you for letting me know about the problem with that report. I am embarrassed and perplexed about how that could happen.
- I appreciate your contacting me immediately about the misinformation in the report.
- I checked the report several times, as did the others on the team. So I was really surprised and embarrassed by the mistake.
- I apologize for the incorrect information in the report. I was really diligent in double-checking the information and getting feedback from others when I had questions.

Then redeem yourself by offering something to compensate for the mistake. Make sure what your offer is equal to the damage you caused. So if the mistake cost a client money or time, try to provide a service at no cost. If the report was for your boss or internal client, demonstrate how you checked your methodology to ensure the mistake won't happen again. Regardless, correct that mistake when possible.

Here are some perfect phrases when settling up with . . .

The Boss

- I'll go back and check the report again and e-mail you a new version on Monday.
- I'll get the team together, and we'll review the report again after work today.
- I will go through my process when compiling the report to determine where I went wrong and avoid a repeat in the future.
- Please know that I strive for accuracy and double-check my facts. I will determine where I went wrong and get back to you immediately.

A Client

- We are embarrassed about the error in our report. We will send you a revision promptly and provide support for the remaining implementation process at no additional charge to you.
- In your e-mail, you requested 10 extra ___ as compensation for the problems. We will gladly provide 15.
- We have reviewed the report closely and will get you a revision first thing on Monday. We will also give you an additional month of our services at no extra expense to you.
- Just to assure you: problems of this rarely occur. In fact, I don't know of another occasion. I would like to meet with you and anyone else from your company to review the corrections and see how we can reconcile this problem moving forward.

Your Coworkers

- I'll review the report again and e-mail all of you a revised copy.
- I'll be happy to correct the other reports to reflect the changes and will send you a copy—on Friday at the latest.
- Sorry about this guys. Just let me know how I can help as we move forward.
- As you know, I've been diligent about checking facts. If anyone has insights about how I could have done this better, I would be most appreciative.

Sometimes, of course, when the mistake wasn't too severe and really just embarrassing, apologize and move on:

- Thanks for pointing out the problem on page 6. I corrected it.
- I appreciate your feedback. Thanks.
- I don't know how that incorrect number got in there. Thanks for pointing it out.
- Many thanks for the correction.

> *Quick tip:* Apologizing is a delicate balance between letting a person know you feel bad about a mistake and treating an ordinary error as a catastrophe. So be careful of overapologizing. You may call more attention to the problem than necessary. Even worse, in some professions, you may even invite a lawsuit. For example, a truck driver at a

company where I consult hit a car accidentally while backing out of an alley. No one was killed, fortunately, but two of the passengers were injured and the car was totaled.

The company received bad press in the local newspapers. Rather than apologize briefly and assure the public that all its drivers were required to attend classes on safe driving skills, the company went on and on and on . . . about the mental and physical pain the passengers must have felt and how heartsick it (as a sensitive company) felt about the issue. This public admission of fault cost the company quite a considerable amount in court.

You Accidentally—but Obviously—Burp, Groan, or Break Wind (It *Does* Happen)

The workplace is about being professional, discreet, and overall, nonhuman. Face it: we have rules of delicacy for everything we do. Rather than gulp down a soda when we've been dying of thirst, we sip it slowly and carefully. Rather than belch, which would feel soooo good, we clamp our lips shut and hold in any unseemly emissions. As for clothes: men wear suits in the blazing heat of summer, and women wear suits or dresses with obligatory sleeves. Should a sweat stain mark the garment, especially beneath the armpits . . . *how embarrassing!*

Okay, let's be reasonable, please. These situations shouldn't be embarrassing any more than breathing should be embarrassing, but there you go. So trust these quick and effective perfect phrases to clean up the mess in these situations.

Situation: You Have Just Broken Wind or Know You're About To

These perfect phrases are especially perfect if you're a guy among a group of guys with a great working relationship. These are usually *not* recommended for mixed company.

- Everyone out! For your own safety! I'm about to let loose.
- Phew. That's disgusting. Did I just do that? Sorry folks.
- Wow! That's a bummer.
- Open the windows! Close your doors!

But remember, this response only works with audiences with that special adolescent sense of humor. Otherwise, go for a more serious and sincere approach:

- Sorry, I've had an upset stomach these days.
- My apologies. What a thing to have happen!
- Sorry guys—I couldn't help it.
- Excuse me.

Situation: You Belch Loudly in Front of a Mixed Crowd

This one is far less offensive, as it disturbs the ears only. So a quick apology will do:

- Sorry, folks.
- Pardon me.
- I beg your pardon.
- Excuse me.
- Yikes—sorry about that.

Situation: You Notice That Your Fly Is Unzipped, Especially in Front of a Crowd When You're the Speaker

Imagine a lecturer at college who was hilarious and wonderful and addressed a least 500 students at a time. And guess what? He spent 90 minutes lecturing on the state of communism in the cold war era with his fly down. What's the best way to handle?

You Can Tell a Joke

- Just getting a little air conditioning.
- Just letting the breeze get in.
- Excuse me—guess I was thinking about this talk when I got dressed today. From now on, I'll pay better attention.

Or Apologize Sincerely

- Pardon me . . .
- Excuse me, would you *(turn and zip)* . . .

Or If You Learn About the Situation Later
You can tie it into a talk the next time you meet to add levity and regain control of the situation. Here are some sample phrases—the actual ones you use should depend on the content of your discussion:

- We must pay attention to details—like, say, unzipped flies.
- Let's make sure the proposal looks fully professional—like an unzipped fly, it will only embarrass us.
- Of course, we're always ready to forgive unwitting indiscretions like, say, an unzipped fly.

Situation: You Have Stains Under Your Arms When Leading a Meeting or during a Presentation

You Can Be Direct

- Seems like the heat is hurting my clothes.
- Pardon my appearance—I know it's not the latest in fashion.

Or Indirect—They'll Get What You Mean

- I sure am hot—are you?
- Boy, is it warm in here!

Or Say Nothing

> *Quick tip:* In mentioning an embarrassing situation after the event, make sure the recipient will have noticed and remembered it. Otherwise, say nothing.

You Call a Person by the Wrong Name

Like so many embarrassing situations, this one doesn't mean a whole lot. No one is hurt. No insult is intended. And life, basically, goes on unchanged. Only the way people respond, you'd never know it! They act like the wrong name—or worse, the wrong pronunciation of their name—is a kick in the face. How dare you! And spell the name wrong? You may as well have publicly humiliated them. So you need to put a few verbal bandages on the sore—with the right perfect phrases, they'll heal in more ways than you think.

When Calling Someone by the Wrong Name in a Meeting or in Introducing Him or Her to a Colleague

- Sorry, you must remind me of someone with that name.
- Yes, of course. Sorry I forgot.
- You remind me of a _____.
- I'm really bad with names, but I remember your face and our previous conversation perfectly.
- Sorry—that's what I meant to say.
- Thanks. I don't know why I got confused.

When Spelling the Name Incorrectly in an E-Mail

- My apologies—I should have known.
- Sorry about incorrectly spelling your name.
- Thanks for correcting my spelling.
- Thanks for the correction. I know someone with your name who spells it differently.
- Thanks for letting me know—I'll spell it correctly from here on in!

When Someone Points Out That You Misspelled a Name in a White Paper, Newsletter, or Blog

■ Thank you for catching that problem. As you can see, I have corrected it on my blog.

■ I appreciate your calling my attention to that mistake.

■ Thanks for letting me know. Amazing how details get away from me.

Mention the mistake—and the correction—in the next publication:

■ We accidentally spelled the mayor's name incorrectly in our blog. It should be _____.

■ In our summer 2008 newsletter, we incorrectly spelled the advisor's name. It should be _____.

■ The name of the ambassador from 1990 to 1996 should have been _____. We will make that correction in future commentaries and publications.

When Mispronouncing Someone's Name

■ Can you say the correct pronunciation again, so I'm sure to get it right this time? *(Repeat the correct pronunciation.)*

■ Sorry. Did you say _____? *(Repeat the correct pronunciation.)*

■ I had no idea. Thank you for telling me.

■ *(Repeat the name.)* Is that correct? Thank you.

When You're Unsure of How to Pronounce Someone's Name—Ask

Better safe than sorry, as the expression goes. Besides, asking for the correct pronunciation of a person's name shows respect, courtesy, and care.

- Could you tell me how to correctly pronounce your name?
- So I get your name right, how do you pronounce it?
- Is this the correct pronunciation of your name: _____
- How do you say your name? I want to be accurate.

Part Three

In the Spotlight—(and Not Sure How You Got There)

These things happen. You're going about your day and suddenly get a call—a colleague just broke his leg—and you need to fill in for him or her at a conference. Or you're setting up for a talk and realize you left your slides back at the office—a six-hour plane ride away. There you are, in the spotlight, with nowhere to hide. Before you make a fool of yourself or otherwise disappoint or disgrace your company, remember these perfect points—then read the perfect phrases for bailing you out of any difficult situation, no matter how glaring the spotlight.

- *Take your time.* Sometimes the spotlight is immediate—like that situation where you're present but the slides are not. Rather than dive ahead, give yourself a moment to strategize about how you'll manage the situation. Admit that you forgot them? Pretend that somehow the airline lost them? Or move into the discussion as if you never intended to use them in the first place?

- *Remain composed.* Regardless of the situation, don't give away your discomfort by fidgeting, sighing loudly, or scratching your face, head, or throat. Instead, stand straight and smile as you make eye contact with one of the participants. But—if you must—engage in a meaningful activity to burn off the energy, such as organizing your paper or preparing a fresh page on the flip chart.

- *Don't overapologize.* The worst thing you can do is draw unwarranted attention to your faux pas. So if the situation does call for an "I'm sorry," say it quickly and move on.

Remember, everyone makes mistakes or doesn't have all the information necessary when others need it. So do the best you can with confidence and control. And remember, don't fidget (see the second bullet point above).

- *Refer them to another authority when appropriate.* Say, someone asks a question and you have no idea about the answer. This is your subject, after all. You should know the answer, right? Give the best answer you can under the circumstance, and refer the person to someone else. Or even better, track down the answer, and e-mail or call later. It will show you're professional and caring. If the press calls about a sticky situation, better have someone from the press room—who can give the right answers in the right way—call back.

- *Follow up. Always follow up.* Forget your slides? Run out of handouts? Have a question from the press you couldn't answer so you sent the reporter to someone else? Doesn't matter—always follow up. Call the press person in your company to make sure he or she connected with your colleague—even if the questions are hostile. This will prove that you're cooperative and have nothing to hide. Forget handouts or slides? Then get the names and addresses of participants at the seminar, and send them a copy. Depending on why you're giving the presentation, this could also prove to be a great business opportunity: send them a note or business card, and tweak their interest in calling you for help.

You're in Front of a Group and Feel Utterly Incompetent—and Unprepared

This happens from time to time—even though you really are a consummate professional, an expert in your field, and a real stand-up performer. Still, you walk in the room thinking you're going to address a group of new (and inexperienced) employees and find yourself facing a group of older and wiser senior VPs. Or you got talked into giving a presentation because you were the most knowledgeable . . . because you knew a little and everyone else in your company knew nothing at all. So there you are, standing at a whiteboard, podium, or Web camera with who knows how many quizzical gazes focusing in on you. What do you do?

When the heat is on, stay cool within by closing your mouth and telling yourself these perfect phrases:

- I can do this—I've done harder things with great success before.
- I know the content inside and out—whatever I say can be helpful.
- I have to trust myself to do the best I can—that's about all I can do.
- This will be a great experience either way.
- People usually like my talks—so the odds are, they'll like this one, too.
- What three things can I do to manage this situation? *(Then give yourself an answer, perhaps starting with "drink some water" or "open by asking them to say what they want from the session.")*

> *Remember:* Don't fidget or fuss. Stand tall, strong, and confident.

Scope Out Your Territory

It's important that you have control over the session. So determine what aspect of the talk you want to focus on—or omit. If that's the case, and you have a PowerPoint presentation, you may have to toss one or two of the slides or briefly touch on the points and then keep going. Just make sure *you* feel comfortable with the direction or territory of your talk.

When introducing the content, be sure to tell your audience what you'll discuss and how they'll benefit from hearing about it:

- You'll be able to apply new models to your business growth with the seven principles we'll review today.
- In today's session, we're going to review ____ so you can ____.
- With the ___ that's we'll cover today, you will get three results.
- The information which I'll review today has helped departments like yours reach these success points.
- With the strategies I'll present today, you will be able to achieve____.
- The information you'll hear in this session is new and unexplored in any way by your competitors.

Be specific to add credibility to your message and better manage your listeners' expectations:

Don't

- You will learn things that will help your organization do better.

- In this seminar, I will cover subject matter that will bring results.

Do

- You will learn seven strategies for accelerating your profitability in the current downturn.

- In this seminar, I will cover strategies from three influential leaders that you can use to grow your business by up to 125 percent within a year.

Establish the Rules

Are you comfortable with people interrupting you with questions? Or would you prefer to answer them all at the end? The organization where you're speaking may have its own preference, but don't worry—you need to establish the rules. This will set you up as an authority and help you take control.

- Please save your questions to the end of the sessions.

- If you have any questions, please wait—I ask to hear them when it makes sense to break.

- I'll take questions just before the break.

- Feel free to ask questions as we go.

- If you have questions, raise your hand, and I'll call on you when we have finished the point.

When You Don't Know the Answer to a Question Either Because It's Not Relevant or You Simply Don't Know

- I'll get back to you about that question later.
- That question is outside of my expertise. I can find the answer and get back to you.
- That's a great question, but I want to address it later. *(Find the answer at your break.)*
- That's a great question, but it doesn't directly address the subject we're covering. Since we don't have much time, I can't address it now. Sorry.
- That question deserves a thorough answer—I'm not quite prepared to address it at this time.

You Don't Have the Required Slides, Handouts, or Other Copy for Your Presentation

People expect goodies when they attend a presentation: a book, handouts, worksheets, tip sheets, and so on. Who knows? Maybe they dump them in the waster later, or maybe they fastidiously take notes in the margin and save them straight through to retirement. Either way, they expect them. And if you don't produce, they feel cheated. Even worse, the distaste will last throughout the session, tingeing their experience no matter how well you do. So here are some steps—with perfect phrases—to make up for the lack—and then some.

Apologize

You have to say something, right? So a quick apology will demonstrate your sincerity. Don't overdo it. Be short and sweet with perfect phrases like these:

- My apologies—I don't have the handouts with me today.
- I'm going to give the talk without slides today. My apologies.
- Sorry—I don't have the handouts with me . . .
- We're going to look at some examples—I'll write them on the whiteboard since I'm sorry to say I don't have the worksheets here today.
- I'm sorry—I didn't pack the support material as I was preparing for this talk.

Avoid Putting Too Glaring a Spotlight on the Mistake, by Not Saying Things Like

Don't say . . .	As in . . .
I forgot	Darn, I forgot to bring the worksheets.
I can't believe . . .	I can't believe I did (or didn't) do this.
Boy am I . . .	Boy am I spacey . . . Boy am I frazzled . . . Boy am I stupid today.
It must be because . . .	It must be because I'm really wiped out. It must be because I'm so busy. It must be because my assistant's out and I can't keep up with details.
I do this . . .	I never do this. I always do this. I do this every time I'm traveling a lot.

Explain When Appropriate

If the reason is good, interesting, and *not* about your emotional or personal state—go ahead. Otherwise, skip this step. The perfect phases will depend on your situation. Here are some examples that can help:

- My suitcase with the handouts never arrived at the airport. Hopefully, I'll get it soon.
- My office was shut down the day before I was leaving, and I couldn't get in to get the notes.
- Someone stole my briefcase at the airport. *(The oldest excuse in the book—but say it if it's true.)*

Promise a Replacement Later—or Even Something Better!

To soothe the pain, however minimal that pain may be, say that you'll send the handouts or the PowerPoint slides. Don't offer—promise, plain and simple. That way you'll have control over the situation and can ensure they won't say no.

Don't Offer

- If you like, I can send you the handouts next week.
- Would you like me to get you those PowerPoints anyway?
- Just give me your e-mail address after the session if you want copies.
- If you still want copies, leave me your e-mail or mailing address, and I'll send them along.

Promise

- I'll get you the handouts first thing next week.
- I'll get you those PowerPoints right away.
- Give me your e-mail address after the session so I can get you the copies.
- Leave me your e-mail or mailing address, and I'll send the copies right away.

If Possible, Explain to Your Audience the Value of Getting the Handouts Late

- You will get the worksheets on Friday. Why not try a few examples: you can test how much you remember and have an easier time applying the information to your work.

- I'll e-mail the PowerPoint presentation so you can add it to your notes.
- I'll send the case studies right away so you can compare them to your situations at work.

Either Way, Avoid Using Negating Terms That Downplay Your Future Actions

Negating terms	As in . . .
The least	The least I can do is e-mail you the worksheets.
Unfortunately . . .	Unfortunately, I'll have to e-mail the case studies later.
Sorry to say . . .	Sorry to say, I can only send them when I return next week.
I cannot . . . until . . .	I cannot get them to you until next week.

When possible—and try to make it possible!—send a little extra. This shouldn't cost you extra, and you'll cash in on lots of goodwill!

Tell your audience what you're sending and how it helps:

- I'm also sending along a series of case studies that will help you apply the content to additional situations.
- I am sending you a copy of a book I wrote so you can see how PR actually helps enhance your customer service.
- In addition, you'll receive a PowerPoint presentation that provides background to today's talk.

You don't have to be direct, by the way. Just be impressive. The content will depend on what you send, of course. Here are a few examples:

- You'll also get a copy of our company president's speech to the Committee on Safety which won accolades from the *New York Times* business section.

- I'm sending you a tape called "Set Yourself Straight: 10 Strategies for Self-Motivation." Over 40,000 people have used the information here to improve their lives and make their fortunes!

Follow Up

You should follow up for lots of reasons. One is to ensure that your audience received your material. Who knows, maybe it got accidentally swallowed up by their spam filter or destroyed by an overly zealous "delete" key. So better check. Also, you want them to remember you—and think highly of you when they do. This could lead to yet another advantage: they may hire you, as a result. But be discreet— you want your follow up to be a sincere inquiry—not a sales pitch.

When Calling
Remind them of who you are:

- I gave the talk _____ at the _____ last week.
- I am the sales rep for _____.
- I was the speaker at the seminar _____.

Tell them what you sent.

- I wanted to make sure you received the slides that I promised plus one of our gold-plated pens.
- Just want to be sure that you received the e-mailed worksheets that I sent on Thursday.
- Please let me know if you received our package on _____ last Tuesday.

When E-Mailing

They know who you are from the letterhead on your e-mail or your e-mail address. So remind them of your talk, and ask whether they received the content.

- Hope you enjoyed the conference in Atlanta and that you received the handouts from my seminar _____.
- Hope you have been well since the seminar last week. Did you get the worksheets that I sent on Wednesday?
- Just to let you know—I sent the case studies from my session _____ on Friday. Please let me know if you received them.

You Need to Prolong a Meeting—or Reconvene One via E-Mail—on a Difficult Topic

This happens more than you'd think. People start fidgeting, your time is up, but you need to keep going. In situations like these, you can't insist that people stay, but you can convince them. Other times, you may need to end the meeting earlier than optimal and must send an e-mail bringing the gang back together. Either way, here are some perfect phrases for taking the edge off a clock that keeps tick-tick-ticking.

When You Know You're About to Go Over

Give them a time frame so they know what to expect, and explain why they should stay. When possible, stress the positive aspect of the situation—especially if controversy, hurt feelings, and even anger may be hovering in the air. Show what you plan to accomplish and why it will ultimately help everyone along.

- We only have 10 more minutes, and I still have two more points I don't want you to miss. So let's go until quarter past the hour; then we'll break.
- Don't start putting your notebooks away yet; we need to go for an extra 10 minutes. Then everyone will know who is responsible for what, and the project should flow smoothly.
- Let's plan to end this session 5 minutes late so I can address all your questions.
- Why don't we keep going until 9:30 so we can address those important issues that ____ and ____ just raised. I think we will all benefit from reviewing them.

- We really need to settle these budget issues before we leave so the project can finally be launched. So let's plan to go until 12:00.
- So we can wrap up with a solid game plan, let's plan to stay for an extra 20 minutes or so.

Quick tip: Give wiggle room to those who need really need to head out, but make sure they get any information they missed:

- If you have a client meeting, I understand that you'll need to go. Just be sure to get notes from one of your colleagues.
- Those of you who take the 3:00 shuttle, go ahead and leave on time. Who can get them the notes?
- If you have a high-priority meeting, go ahead, but find someone who will give you meeting notes.
- If you must leave, be sure to get a list of our goals for next week; you'll be responsible either way.
- We'll be giving out assignments at the end of the meeting; if you need to go, I understand, but we'll assign you a responsibility.

You're Over the Time Limit and Want to Keep Them from Leaving

Think *limit, purpose*.

Limit	**Purpose**

- Could you guys wait 10 more minutes? We have an important decision to make.
- We only need about 10 more minutes, and your input on the proposal will be critical.
- Hold on everyone—we need ten more minutes or so to come to a conclusion before everyone leaves.
- We can't stop yet—we need at least 15 more minutes, or we'll lose our momentum.

You Need to Finish the Session Another Time

Be definite about when you're meeting next—or how you intend to reach people to decide.

Don't

- We didn't complete everything—we'll need to meet again.
- Someone will be back in touch with you to figure out a good time to finish this up.
- Let's get together and finish this discussion sometime soon.

Do

- We need more time to cover everything—please mark your calendars for the same time and place next week.
- We need to complete our goals list. _____, will you get back to everyone tomorrow about the time that works best?

- We have to complete this budget by Monday. Send me a time that works best for you on Friday morning, and I'll figure something out.
- Let _____ know tomorrow whether you can meet next Thursday. If not, we'll meet on Friday, but no later.
- We need to reconvene on Thursday at 2:00. If you can't make it, let me know. But because of time issues, you'll lose your vote.

You Need to Reconvene the Meeting through an E-Mail

Remind them of the last meeting, what you need to complete your agenda, and when you're holding it:

- Since we ran out of time at the May 14 meeting, we still need to determine the budget for our project. So we will meet again on May 21 at 3:00 in the _____ Conference Room.
- Our goal for the all-hands meeting was to determine an implementation strategy for_____. While we came up with some great ideas, we still need to develop a concrete strategy. Let _____know when you are available next week.
- At the May 19 meeting, we decided to contact _____ with a finished proposal. So that we can stick to our plan, we will need to meet on Tuesday.
- As you know, we ran over time at Tuesday's meeting. So that we can determine next steps and keep the program on track, we must meet again this Tuesday.

Quick tip: Use positive language, focusing on what *can* happen, rather than what didn't happen. This can project a feeling of optimism—especially important when people are feeling disgruntled or otherwise grim. Notice the subtle but important difference:

Don't

- We didn't finish allocating the budget.
- We never clarified the correct procedure in those situations.
- Mary didn't get an answer to her last question.

Do

- We need to finish allocating the budget.
- We must clarify the correct procedure in those situations.
- Mary should get an answer to her last question.

Your Colleagues Ask You to Address a Situation That You Know the Audience Won't Like

Well, someone's got to do it, as the old saying goes. And why shouldn't it be you? Okay, you can think up a dozen reasons why it *shouldn't* be you: maybe you're not qualified, maybe the situation is just too complicated, or maybe you simply don't like controversy. You have enough headaches, right? But there you are on the hot seat—and face it, everyone gets there some time. These perfect phrases should help cool you down—and will help you with addressing other tense situations, too.

When Addressing the Controversial Issue in an E-Mail

It's always best to address a difficult situation in person; you can look at the audience's response, see their reactions, and manage your comments according to how they feel. If they look alarmed, for example, you can put them at ease with a comment, a smile, or a sympathetic look. Not so with writing. They may be shrieking with rage or nodding with sad understanding—how would you know, though? So your best option would be to ask them for a time when you can discuss the situation face-to-face. Here are some perfect phrases that can help.

Subject Line
Keep the subject line fast and informative; you want them to pay attention and open your e-mail, but you *don't* want them to be alarmed. Use strong verbs and a forward-looking approach when possible—or just ask for a meeting:

- Project X changes
- Can we meet on Monday?
- New information on ___
- New directions for ___
- Plan changes—can we discuss?
- Meeting about developments—Thursday?

First Line

This line will set a tone for the rest of your e-mail. Try not to be too gloomy or alarmist—remember, you need to keep your audience's confidence so that they'll respond in the calmest, most effective way:

- We have just learned of changes to the project ___ that we need to discuss.
- I was hoping to meet you early next week to discuss some recent matters regarding our budget.
- We have just gathered some important information about our project for ___.
- We need to adapt our timeline for the ___.
- ___ called earlier today; he has some important information that I would like to discuss with you.

Body of the Message

Add any details that might be helpful—but not too many. Remember, your mission is to get them to meet with you ASAP so you can spill the beans in the most productive way—not to dump information they won't like. Make sure the recipients know their role in the discussion:

- The _____ has changed their mind about several aspects of the project, and we need to discuss what our next steps should be.
- The funding has shifted on several fronts, which I can tell you about in detail.
- We need to make several changes to our timeline. I would like to review these with you before taking any steps.
- We need to make some decisions regarding these changes.

Sometimes, you may need to forget the body of the e-mail altogether and just ask for the meeting.

Closing

This is where you make the concrete plans. Be as specific as possible, and provide additional information, such as your office or cell phone, when necessary.

- Can you meet tomorrow morning to discuss?
- I will be in town on Monday and would like to see you then. You can e-mail me or reach me on my cell at_____.
- When is the best time for us to meet this week?
- Would you and ____ be available to meet on March 14? If you want to discuss some options and I'm not available, please contact my assistant, _____. He has my schedule and will find a time that works best for you.

Sometimes, of course, you have to deliver the bad news electronically. Keep your subject and first lines more or less the same as when you're requesting a meeting, but change the rest using perfect phrases like these.

Body of the Message

Give them boundaries for the discussion so they know what's ahead. So, for example, you might say:

- We have three issues that cropped up recently that we must address. First . . .
- Within the next few weeks, we are going to address these unexpected changes . . .
- Because of _____, we need to make five small changes to your original plan.
- The budget will be higher than we originally predicted for these two reasons:

Then let them know how you plan to address the situation:

- Our next step is to give you a revised plan.
- We will continue moving ahead in spite of these changes.
- Our team will meet on Tuesday and have the changes to you, in writing, on Wednesday.
- We will meet with our accountants on Monday to determine the most expedient ways to minimize the expenses.

Closing

Regardless of the future, make sure your recipients are clear about when they will hear from you again. This will give them the sense you're in control.

- We will contact you after the meeting on Monday to fill you in.
- I will call you on Thursday to ensure you got the package.

- After I send you the new financial plan, I'll call to see if you have questions.
- We will be back with you about these changes the minute we know more—the 10th at the latest.

When Addressing the Controversial Issue in a Meeting

Start out warmly—letting the participants feel somehow special (in spite of the message you're about to deliver):

- I think it's important that you know . . .
- We thought you should be the first ones to hear about . . .
- We're pretty sure the media will get hold of this soon, and we wanted you to know directly from us . . .
- I know that people are gossiping a lot and thought you should know the facts.

Then tell them the bad news.

When Your Group Dropped the Ball Somehow
Tell them what happened—obviously this depends on your situation, but the phrases should be direct and quick:

- We needed to back up the information on our computer, and when the hard drive died, we lost the information.
- Our subcontractor made an error and will have to lay the foundation again.
- Our company president was involved in insider trading, and the media's about to find out.
- Our predictions were off by _____.

Then tell them what you plan to do next. Where possible, highlight any advantages they get from the mishap:

- We will reenter the information over the next two weeks. This will give us an opportunity to fact-check again and take out antiquated or irrelevant information.
- He will double-check the measurements and use the right _____.
- We're going to put together a really strong PR campaign that will underscore the ethical nature of our group, otherwise.
- Ultimately, we will have more access to the trends.

Depending on the response, periodically ask if they have questions. This will give them a sense of control and the feeling that you're not withholding information from them:

- If anyone has any questions, please ask.
- I welcome all your questions.
- If you have questions, please raise your hand and I'll call on you.
- I'm eager to take your questions. If you don't have enough time, please contact me after the meeting.
- I'd like to answer all your questions—if you have any after the meeting ends, please e-mail me.

Quick tip: Try to avoid language that aggravates the situation. For example, don't use unnecessary modifiers in cases like these:

Avoid	**As in**
Only	We only reached four of our five goals.

| Just | You will receive just half of the report. |
| Unfortunately | Unfortunately, we didn't expect that shift. |

Also, try not to add value judgments; your audience will make their own assertions.

Avoid	**As in**
Terrible	The only way we can address this terrible situation . . .
Miserable	We must address this miserable turn of events . . .
Unfortunate	Because of this unfortunate situation . . .
Pathetic	The pathetic results prove that . . .

An Employee Turns to You for Help When a Customer Starts Complaining—Loudly—in the Lobby of Your Business

This situation is unsettling for everyone—you, your employee, the person who is carrying on, everyone else in the lobby, and those friends and family members who get to hear all about it later. So it's up to you to diffuse the difficult situation immediately. First step: your demeanor. True, you're cringing inside, but let your face reveal nothing but calm control. You've addressed worse—hey, this is a piece of cake. Okay, a bitter piece of cake, but still. Then use these perfect phrases—usually in the order that you'll find them here.

Calm the Customer

- Excuse me, is there a problem that I can help you with?
- Pardon me, do you think we could talk?
- I couldn't help overhearing that you were upset. I'd like to talk with you about it.

Remember: If you've ever been in an argument with a spouse or child, telling an upset person to calm down can have the opposite effect—he or she will get even more excited. So best to avoid that suggestion, and instead assure the customer that you can work out the problem:

- I'm sure we can figure this out.
- I'd like to know the problem to see if we can solve it.
- If you're having problems with one of the employees here, I think we should address the issue.
- Let's figure out what we can do to help.

Request That the Employee Speak to You Privately

- Why don't you come in my office, and we'll discuss this together?
- How about sitting on the chair over there, and we'll talk.
- Why not sit in the break room, and we'll have a cup of coffee?
- If you don't have time to talk now, feel free to contact me if you want to talk later.

Calm the Employee

Often, you need to disengage the customer without making the employee look foolish in the eyes of everyone else. So be sure to address the employee with trust, familiarity, and calm. Frequently, a simple word or two will do—call the employee by his or her name when possible to show that you connect.

- Thanks, _____.
- You okay, _____? Great.
- We'll figure this out, _____. Go ahead back to work.
- I'll talk to you later, _____.

At a Meeting, Participants Ask You to Explain a Scandal That Occurred at Your Company

When a scandal or related difficult situation occurs at work, you know it's not your fault. You didn't lie; your CEO did. You didn't have the affair; your boss did. And you didn't deceive the shareholders; that was the company president. Yet you, who were busy doing your job, suddenly get asked about the scandal at a meeting, during a sales pitch, or in the middle of a presentation. You do represent the company, right? So now what? Like anything else, be sure to project composure and willingness to talk by using these perfect phrases.

Thank Them for Asking or Bringing the Issue Up

Politicians do this all the time—but don't let that detail stop you. Thanking them will underscore your openness, lack of concern about the event, and willingness to talk. Besides, you really *do* appreciate their asking, right? After all, it gives you a chance to address what's on everyone's mind in a way that works to your advantage.

- Thanks for bringing this up. I'd like to address this situation.
- I appreciate your raising this issue—I'm sure everyone's thinking about it.
- Good thing you brought this up—I'm sure just about everyone wanted to.
- I wasn't about to raise the issue so I'm glad you brought it up.
- I appreciate the chance to discuss what's going on.
- Yes, this just came out in the news—do all of you know what happened? *(If not, explain in the most factual way possible.)*

Distance Yourself from the Situation

- I know about as little as you do.
- I was surprised, too, to tell you the truth.
- This situation doesn't affect anyone in my department.
- Since no one in my department was involved, we know very little about it.
- I only heard a few things, which I'll be happy to share with you. *(Obviously, these are* not *damaging or confidential.)*
- There's been quite a lot of speculation, but the service you receive will remain unchanged.
- Try to do what I do—don't trust rumor or speculation. Just see what's immediately in front of you. In my case, the coast will be clear.

Tell Them What They Can Expect—the Best and the Worst—to Manage Their Expectations

Worst

- I'm sure you'll hear lots on the media from now on.
- Our stocks may go down in the short run, but they'll bounce back, I can assure you.
- No question, people will be talking. But don't always trust what you hear.
- People always read the worst into these things . . .

Best

- We're a resilient group, and I'm sure this will blow over.
- This may mean we'll need to make changes—but trust me, they'll be for the better.

- Even if the _____ should happen, we'll survive. This has happened before, and look where we are now.
- Normally, events like these just make us stronger.

Do Not

- Speculate about why the situation happened.
- Express concern.
- Apologize for the event.
- Speak confidentially about the situation.
- Speak disparagingly about anyone you know who was involved.

Do

- Create an unbiased impression.
- Remain respectful of your company.
- Accentuate your role as a professional—not a spokesperson.
- Avoid making any judgments—good or bad.

A Newspaper Asks You to Discuss a Problem Confronting Your Industry

Unless you're in PR, you shouldn't be addressing questions from newspapers, even from your local college rag. But now and then, you'll find yourself in a difficult situation where a reporter asks about the market, your company's stand on an industry issue, or another matter. So, yes, you need to address the situation, if only to (politely and strategically) walk away. These perfect phrases will open the door for a clean exit.

When the Journalist First Asks the Question

- You need to talk to our PR Department. If you go online, you'll find the number.
- As a _____, I'm not privy to that kind of information, nor can I comment on it.
- If you want to know about that situation, go to the Q&A on our Web site. It has answers.
- Those are all very good questions. Why not contact _____?
- If you e-mail me later, I'll get you the right name of a source for your article.

If the Journalist Persists

Stay friendly and calm, so you don't look like you have something to hide:

- I'm sorry, but you'll need to contact _____ at our press room, as I mentioned.
- Lots of people are asking lots of questions. But as I said, I don't have any answers to give.

- I'd love to clarify these issues, but I simply don't have much to offer at this point.
- I'd love to answer your questions, but right now, I am not able to do so.

When You've Agreed to Meet with the Media

Sometimes you are willing to accept an interview. But the questions might put you in a difficult bind, like when you're asked to speak poorly about your boss. Here are some perfect comebacks that should get you off the hook:

- I can't speak to that.
- That isn't relevant to the discussion.
- I'll pass on that question. What else would you like to ask?
- No comment. Next question.
- I have nothing to say to that.

You're the Point Person for a Problem or Other Difficult Situation—but You're Not Sure Why

Maybe the problem originated with your group. Maybe the person in charge is out, so you're filling in. Either way, there you are, the point person with no answers to give. Here are some perfect phrases so you project a sense of control and can avoid dispensing information that's really conjecture or an old-fashioned guess.

When You Need to Pass the Buck

Be clear that you're sending them to the best possible person: one who's so high up the ladder, there's no place better for them to go.

- I'd like to help, but _____ is really a better person.
- The best person for you to talk about this is _____.
- Why don't you give _____ a call and get back to me about what happens.
- I know a little about the situation, but _____ knows more. Why not contact her this week?

  When possible, directly make the connection:

- _____ is our senior most person in that area. He will be able to help you. I'll e-mail her and cc you to make the connection.
- I'll call _____ to let him know that we talked and fill him in on our discussion. Then you can get in touch with him early next week.
- I'll give _____ a call and have her call you. What time works best?

- I received your e-mail about _____ and forwarded it to _____. He is our expert in that area and will get in touch with you tomorrow.

Be specific whenever possible. Obviously, the particulars will depend on the content you're discussing, but here are some ideas:

- _____ in our Accounting Department will get back to you about the correct way you should have filled out that form and will tell you what you can do to repair the damage.
- I'll have _____ send you the three steps you need to take to get back on track.
- _____ is in our Legal Department and knows the best way for you to respond. Please wait for her to contact you before e-mailing or talking to anyone about the matter. If you don't hear from her, notify me and I'll be in touch.
- You'll need to learn more about your options before you progress. E-mail _____, who will send them to you.

When You Need to Get More Information and Get Back to Them

Be sure *not* to suggest that you don't know what you're doing, that someone made a mistake in passing your name along, or that you're junior level. This will only create more anxiety and make your life harder—and everyone else's, too.

Don't

- I really have no idea.
- Why would they send you to me? I'm not even in the right department.

- How on earth would I know?
- Honestly, I don't know. This just isn't my area of expertise.
- Huh?
- Who sent you to me—and why?
- Wish I could help you, but you're out of luck.

Do

- I'd like to get more information before I give a response.
- Let me check on a few things, and I'll be back in touch.
- I have a few points I need to clarify before I address this situation.
- This is interesting—let me get back to you so I get all the details straight.
- I'd like to ask my colleague about this; he is an expert and will be able to provide the best information.

Always give them a precise day, time, and communications vehicle—otherwise, they'll feel like you shoved them to the backburner where they'll languish, forgotten.

- I'll get back to you within 24 hours.
- Once I hear from her, I'll e-mail you.
- I'll e-mail you one way or the other within a week.
- I'll cc ___ on the e-mail and follow-up first thing on Friday.

Whenever possible, use the first person plural "we" instead of the second person "you." This shows that you feel personally involved in helping them solve the problem:

- I'll call _____. We should get precisely the right information from him.
- _____ is really helpful. She'll get back to us quickly.

- I think we should be able to solve this problem by the end of the week.
- We shouldn't have trouble getting the updates you need—let me get back to you with specifics.

When the Person Contacting You Is Upset

A person who's upset usually can't grasp what you're saying no matter how conciliatory you're trying to be. If someone sent that person to you, the plot only thickens; chances are the person's been talking to other people and the frustration has been mounting and mounting.

Reassure the person, and then ask for the information:

- Well, you came to the right place. Why don't you tell me what happened?
- Okay, well don't you worry; I'm going to help you. Why don't you start at the beginning?
- I'm so glad that you contacted me. I'll make sure you get the right answers. What exactly is going on?
- Thank you for contacting me. I know we can figure this out—so why don't you tell me what happened.
- Let's figure this out. Tell me the problem—don't leave out any details.

If you don't understand what the person is saying, ask for clarification. Make sure he or she knows you're asking so you can be helpful—not because you aren't informed or concerned.

- Can you give me details so I'm clear about what you're saying?
- Let me ask you a few questions so I know precisely what is going on.

- I want to be clear about what you just said—can you repeat that last point?
- Please repeat what you just said so I'm sure of the details.
- I have a few questions I want to ask before you continue . . .

Make sure you know precisely what the person wants as an outcome—since you're outside your area of expertise, this may not be apparent.

- What exactly do you need?
- How can I help you?
- In what ways can I help resolve the situation for you?
- What would you like to have happen now?
- It sounds like you need the following three things to happen . . .

You Need to Discuss a Problem with a Boss When a Friend, Colleague, or Employee Dropped the Ball

This person is usually a great worker, and you don't want to ruin his or her credibility.

You're in a bind that requires absolute discretion. You don't want to accuse a good worker of being irresponsible or of being a bad worker. Most certainly you don't want the person's bonus or promotion potential to be affected, either. Yet that person must be accountable. So what do you do? Here are some answers.

Be Objective

It's important that you state your point as fairly as possible. So rely on facts—what happened from a purely objective perspective. How do you know if it's objective? Essentially, you can measure or otherwise prove it. When you're objective, you give a clear idea of what went wrong and what you (or someone) can do to correct the situation—with no judgment involved. So avoid terms that reflect a value, and get straight to the point.

Do Not

- _____ did something really stupid . . .
- Yesterday, _____ was rude to a customer in the lobby.
- _____ made a ridiculously empty-headed mistake.
- _____ really dropped the ball.
- I couldn't believe what happened.

Do

The actual phrases will depend on your circumstances—here are some examples:

- _____ deleted the files with the account in it.
- Yesterday, _____ told a customer to shut up.
- _____forgot to lock the safe.
- _____ didn't complete the proposal.
- The following is what happened from my vantage point . . .

Show Desired Outcome

- _____ needs to reload the files as quickly as possible.
- _____ needs to go to a customer service training course.
- We need to put up reminders on the safe.
- _____ needs to be responsible for completing all proposals in the future.
- _____ needs to ensure that type of situation doesn't occur again.

Remind the Boss That This Behavior Was Unusual, but Do Not Use Negative Terms That Describe the Person

- ____ is usually so smart about things.
- ____ normally has a great way with people.
- ____ is really security-minded.

Do rely on factual or observable information:

- A situation like this never happened before.
- ____ is usually polite and appropriate.
- ____ has never had a security breech before this.

Part Four

When Personal Tragedies Flare Up at Work

The workplace is about professional and nonpersonal relationships. Sure, we talk about our kids, our aspirations, and what we did for vacation, but we don't get into great detail. That's not the point of being at work—or of having work relationships. But now and then, you have no option but to mix the personal and professional, especially when a colleague has suffered a tragedy.

Communicating about these issues is harder to do than most people think. You have to mix emotional factors with logistical ones. You must slow down and consider someone else's feelings or life situation . . . without missing deadlines or slowing the pace of work. And you must be sympathetic without being syrupy or inappropriate. It is a hard balance to achieve, indeed. So what should you do? Read through these pointers. Then we'll look at difficult situations and perfect phrases for addressing them.

- *Show, don't tell.* Objectively describe the event that is occurring rather than explain how horrible, sad, or mind-boggling the situation is. This is the fundamental difference between showing and telling. When telling, you explain the situation from your point of view and hope people agree. When showing, you let people see the situation for themselves and come up with the right conclusions.

  Notice the difference here—you'll see more as you review the perfect phrases in this section:
  Show: He needs back surgery that will keep him in traction for a few weeks.

Tell: He has to undergo painful and exhausting surgery to his back.

- *Be precise about the future.* If your coworker is ill, say that you or others will fill in during his or her absence. When contacting others, tell them how long your coworker will be out and specifically how they can help.

  Don't: We'll need to take on _____'s tasks while she is out of work.

  Do: We'll need to e-mail the billings and check for delayed payments for the next two days.

- *Comment only on what's apparent.* It's critical that you give your coworker the right to privacy and the space to express—or not express—his or her feelings. And yes, it's always nice to sympathize; just sympathize in an appropriately limited way:

  Don't: I'm sure that's really uncomfortable, especially when you go to the bathroom.

  Do: I'm sorry to hear you're in pain.

A Colleague Is Diagnosed with a Serious Illness

This situation may be the most sensitive of them all. A colleague learns difficult news that brings promises of pain and, probably, mandatory time off. You don't want to pry, but you don't want to seem insensitive or uncaring. So here's what you do.

Express Concern

Chances are, your colleague is nervous and, quite possibly, feeling the need for privacy. So use these perfect phrases to address the situation—then let your colleague talk or not, depending on what he or she feels most comfortable doing.

When Someone Else Told You About the Illness

- _____ told me you were ill. I hope you're not feeling too badly.
- I just heard that you were feeling badly and wanted to check in.
- Are you feeling okay? I just heard you were diagnosed with _____.
- I don't want to pry or embarrass you, but I heard you were unwell and wanted to express my concern.

When Your Colleague Told You About His or Her Illness

- I'm sorry to hear that.
- What a surprise. Thank you for telling me.
- That's too bad. How do you feel?
- So sorry to hear about the diagnosis.

When Appropriate, Offer Encouragement

- You look so healthy, though. I'm sure you can beat it.
- You've always taken such good care of yourself; I know you have the power to resist it.
- I know you're smart enough to get the right help to overcome this illness.
- I've heard that doctors have made major strides in curing this illness.
- They have all sorts of new medications that can help.

> *Quick tip:* If you know someone who contracted the illness and survived, you can mention it. Knowing others have gone through the difficult situation can be helpful.

Offer Support

Often, open-ended offers of support help people feel cared for but not intruded on:

- Can I help in any way?
- What can I do for you?
- Anything you need?
- How can I assist you?

Yet they can also sound insincere. So whenever possible, be specific:

- Since you won't be able to drive, let me know if I can take you to work.

- If you need me to cover for you in the mornings, just let me know.
- I can complete the report if you're not up to it.
- Just e-mail me if you need any of the office files while you're working at home.
- I can arrange conference calls when you're ready, so you can keep abreast of the project.

Ask Whom You Can Tell

- If you want me to contact anyone at work, let me know. I'll be happy to do so.
- Do you want me to tell your team anything or have them call you?
- Whom would you like me to contact for you?
- Would you mind if I e-mailed the members of your team? I know they care about you and would want to hear.

Check In from Time to Time

Whether you send an e-mail or call on the telephone is up to you. These perfect phrases work in both instances:

- I was checking to see how you were feeling.
- Just wanted to know how you're doing.
- We miss you here at work and wanted to check in.
- So what's going on—we want you back in the office.
- Everyone on the team wants to know when you're coming back. We miss you.

Use Humor When Appropriate

- Since you've been out, our department has basically fallen apart. When will you be back? (We need you!)

- We have this little vacuum at your desk—everyone's waiting for you to get back and fill it. (The breeze is making us cold!)

Quick tip: When should you initiate an e-mail or a phone call? E-mails give your audience a chance to absorb the message—or leave it aside—at their own pace. Besides, e-mails don't require anything from the recipients. They read it and aren't obligated to respond outside of hitting the reply button and saying something like "Thanks." Still, e-mails can seem less formal and less interactive. As for the telephone, if you have a strong or joking relationship, calls can help draw a warm and important connection. Which you use when contacting an employee with a serious illness depends on the employee's preference, his or her state of mind, and your relationship.

An Employee Must Take Leave Because of a Health Problem

Communicating with this person—whether you're a friend, project manager, or boss—can be tricky. You need to be sympathetic without yielding beyond the call of duty. You need to make professional decisions about how to distribute work because of highly personal matters. And you need to spread the word without breaking confidentiality. These perfect phrases will help you strike a balance between all these factors to keep the workplace stable.

What to Say When the Employee Gives You the News

Express Personal Concern

- I'm really sorry to hear that you'll be out.
- I hope you recover quickly.
- Sorry you won't be here; hopefully, you'll be feeling great soon.
- I'm sorry to hear about this problem. How can we help?
- Are you feeling okay?

Remember: Be careful not to overdo the sympathy, in spite of your best intentions. And don't make any promissory statements, especially in writing. Should problems arise, these will work against you.

Don't

- How awful—please, take as much time as you need to recover. We'll fill in for you, no problem, and your place will be here when you return.

- Health problems can really be debilitating. I'll understand if you need to take a leave for weeks longer than you predict.

- This is tough mentally and physically. Good thing you work for a company like ours that has such a good health plan and understanding leave policies.

Do

- Just let us know how much time your doctor says you'll need to recover.

- Be sure to take really good care of yourself while you're off recovering.

- I know this isn't easy, but everyone here is eager for a fast recovery.

Discuss Logistical Matters

- How much time did the doctor say you need to recover?

- Are you planning to work from home? If so, when do you think you can start?

- What kinds of work will you be able to do from your house when you're ready?

- When do you think you'll be able to return to work part time? Full time?
- We need to get a list of all your projects and your progress in each of them. What is the best way to do this?
- I'd like some input about who should fill in on your key projects. When will be the best time for you to do this?
- Would you like to listen in to our meetings on a conference call? If so, I'll be happy to arrange that.

Settle on a Plan

- So here's what we can expect over the next two months . . .
- Here's our game plan through April . . .
- Let me know what you think of this arrangement . . .
- Make sure we have your contact numbers, in case we need you, and the best times to call . . .

Determine What You Can and Cannot Say to Other People

- I need to tell people that you'll be out. What would you like me to tell them?
- I'd like to tell your clients that you'll be gone for a while. Would you like me to write an e-mail on your behalf and show you before it goes out? Or would you like to write one yourself?
- People will be asking questions. How much detail can I give them?
- Do you want people to know that you have _____, or should I just tell them that you're sick and leave it at that?
- People here really care about you, as you know. So what can I tell them so they don't worry too much?
- Can I give people your home e-mail for personal correspondences?

What to Say to Others in the Workplace or on Your Team

Yes, you may be aching to give away details about the employee's ailment, especially when it underscores that the employee really does need to stay home recovering. But confidentiality is key, so better not. Instead, use the perfect phrases.

Be Factual

- ____ will be out for a while because he is ill. The doctor says we should see him in three to four weeks, though.
- ____ contracted _____. The situation looks good, but she will need to take a few weeks off.
- ____ just told me he will need to be out on sick leave for the next two months.
- _____ needs to take another leave because of ____. We expect her to return in the fall.

When appropriate, let others know how they may be affected from a health perspective:

- This isn't contagious, so you won't have to worry about your own health.
- This is contagious, so if you notice a skin irritation that won't go away, contact your doctor.
- Whether or not this is contagious, no one seems to know—even specialists. You can find a list of warning signs on the Web.
- It's possible she contracted the illness from eating bad food. Since no one in the company has this problem, though, we assume the food in the cafeteria is fine.

- As you know, the problem isn't contagious and is, most likely, hereditary. You should go to your doctor for a screening, though, to detect any problems early.

Discuss Logistical Matters

- We need to look at his project list to divide up responsibilities.
- All of us need to take one of her assignments, and we should cover them all.
- I'll review his responsibilities and assign whichever ones can't wait for his return.
- I have a list of _____'s projects. Most of the steps here can wait, but I'll need to assign some of you extra tasks to cover. You'll hear from me early next week.
- I have a list of assignments that will help cover for _____ when she is out. Please review them and build them into your schedule of events.

If one person will have to share the bulk of the responsibility, be sure all the members of your team know they must provide support:

- _____ must take on these responsibilities since she shares many of these clients. However, we should all be available to pitch in.
- I appreciate _____'s willingness to take on these responsibilities. How can the rest of us help?
- I know that _____ has more than his share of responsibilities to cover for _____ while she is out. So if _____ is in a crunch, let's all agree to pitch in any way we can.

Let your coworkers know that you appreciate their efforts to pitch in:

- I really appreciate your helping out with this. No one expected that ____ would be out this long.
- I know you guys are swamped with work as it is. So I doubly appreciate your willingness to help ___ while he is out.
- Thank you all for being so helpful at this time. In the long run, everyone including our customers will benefit from your efforts.
- Thanks so much for pitching in. I can't even imagine how bad things would get if you hadn't.

What to Say When Others Protest the Employee's Absence

The absence is not optional or a sign of the employee's irresponsibility. So everyone else will simply have to live with it. State this as matter-of-factly as you can:

- ____ is sick. No one asked for that to happen, least of all ____. So we have to do our best.
- This is a difficult time, and we must get behind ____ until he is well enough to return.
- We need to pull together to take on additional responsibilities without letting other things slide. So let's look at what we can do to keep things going, rather than complain.
- I don't want to hear complaints, at this time. I would like to hear ideas, though, about what we can do to make this transition easier.
- Why doesn't everyone write down one or two ways you can help fill in for ____ and read them aloud. Then we'll work together to find the best steps for moving ahead.

A Colleague's Partner or Parent Dies

Obviously, death is something no one can respond to in quite the right way. The loss can be overwhelming, and yet life needs to go on. You need to acknowledge the pain your colleague is confronting—while clarifying logistical issues. How you do this can occur in stages—from a day or so after the death occurred to a week or so from the funeral. Here are some perfect phrases to help.

When First Learning About the Death of a Parent

Mention how you learned about the event, and share whatever knowledge or memories you have to underscore your sincerity:

- _____ just told me that your mother passed away. I was so sorry to hear about it. I know the two of you were quite close.
- Thank you for letting me know about your father's passing. I understand that he was sick for some time; still, this must be difficult for you.
- Sorry to hear that your mother passed away so suddenly. This must be a terrible shock.
- I just learned that your father passed away yesterday. I know you were such a close family; this must be a real shock to you all.
- So sorry to hear that your mother died. I remember meeting her at the conference last year. She was a funny and spirited woman.
- Sorry to hear about your father. He was a learned man: I was most impressed when I met him at your daughter's wedding.

When First Learning About the Death of a Partner

Because the death of a spouse or partner can have an immediately devastating effect, make yourself as present and available as is appropriate for your relationship:

- I was surprised and saddened to learn about ____. Please know I'm thinking about you constantly and will be happy to help in any way I can.
- _____, I was so sorry to learn that ____ passed away. If there is anything I, or anyone in my family, can do for you and the kids, please let me know.
- I was so sad to hear about ____. I know this must be hard; I hope you realize everyone here feels for you.

Clichés diminish the sincerity of any message—none quite so much as a condolence note. So avoid some of the clichés you might find on a greeting card, and opt for the specifics, as you can see in the examples above.

Phrases to Avoid

- My deepest condolences for your loss.
- Our thoughts are with you.
- May she rest in peace.
- My deepest sorrow for your loss.
- My sympathies at this great time of loss.

When Addressing Return-to-Work Issues When the Grieving Person Is Still at Home

Be specific about what you need, and let them know that you understand:

- Can you let us know about when you'll be returning to work? There is no hurry. We just need to know so we can best accommodate you.
- I want you to know we respect your need to be with your family. If you have a sense of when you'll return to work, that would be helpful to us. But please, no rush.
- We all miss you at work but understand if you need to take another week off. Just let us know if you want to come back sooner.
- As you know, our employee policy states that you get a week of leave. But everyone here is willing to pitch in if you need extra time.

When Asking for Information About Materials at Work

- I know this is a hard time for you and respect your need to be with your family. If possible, could you tell me the password for your computer? We are covering for you so when you return to work, the transition back will be smooth.
- I don't want to intrude on your privacy but was hoping we could talk for a few minutes. I need to find _____. Could you give me a call or e-mail about the best time for me to call you?
- I know this is a time when you'll want privacy. Do you think you could e-mail me? If you would like to speak on the phone, just let me know.

An Employee Must Miss Work Because a Parent or Child Is Sick and Requires Attention

Having a sick child or parent is traumatic and most certainly a valid reason for an employee to take time off work. But through the back-and-forth of caring for the sick family member, the employee will also have reprieves: time to make a call, answer e-mails, and otherwise catch up with life. Many employees value this time; they can connect with peers and think about their own, independent lives. So while you obviously need to be empathetic, don't be afraid to ask how much time, if any, an employee can dedicate to work.

When First Hearing the News

Because the person is sick, but not mortally ill, express understanding and hope:

- I hope ___ gets better soon.
- Sorry to hear about ____. Hopefully, she will be up and about soon.
- _____ told me that ____ has been sick. Tell him I said to hurry up and get well.

When Discussing Timing

As you can see, the last set of perfect phrases is easy, if not obvious. But now you have to ask how long the employee will be out, without actually rushing him or her. These perfect phrases should help:

- Do you have a sense of how much time you'll need to be away?

- Do you know when you'll be able to get your mother into a nursing home?
- Do you know when you will be able to return to work full time?
- Will you need to be out of work until plans to care for your father are established?
- How long do you suppose the treatment will last?
- We need to make plans so members of the team can fill in while you're gone. I know these things can take time, but how long do you think you'll be absent?

When Asking Whether the Employee Can Work from Home

You may need to ask whether the person can devote time to work in a general sense:

- Think you can help us out while you're at home?
- Will you be available through e-mail?
- Do you think you can contact us in the afternoons in case we have questions or need some advice?

If the situation isn't dire, such as a child has a cold, you may use assumptive language, where you assume the person will work from home:

- When will you be available if we need help?
- What is the best way to reach you—by e-mail or phone?
- Which project will you be taking home with you?

When possible, see if the person can commit to concrete projects. This will put clear expectations on how much, or little, of a contribution you can expect.

- Will you have any time in the morning to discuss the project plan?
- Could you try to complete the budget by Friday?
- Can you work with ___ over the phone to finish _____?

> *Quick tip:* Try not to get the person to commit to a certain number of hours. If interrupted or otherwise distracted, he or she may not have a clear sense of time. Then the person will (honestly) claim he or she worked for three hours but only completed one hour's worth of work. The exception, of course, is when the person is paid an hourly fee.

You Are Experiencing Personal Problems and Need Flexibility at Work

When enduring a personal crisis, the last thing you want is to determine strategies for taking time off work. But you can't simply *not* show up. So you need to contact your boss, colleagues, and possibly your clients, letting them know in the most professional way possible that a personal issue is, essentially, mucking up your life. Be clear before you start about how much time you'll need; what other people must do to fill in for you; and when you will be available in terms of hours and times of day, should they need help.

When introducing the subject, explain the situation—you can be general:

- _____ is sick, and I need to take care of him.
- _____ has left the family, and I need some time to work things out.
- I just learned that _____ and will have to fly to _____ to sort things out.
- I'll need to take a leave of absence for a few months because_____.
- _____'s doctor just told us that she needs to go into the hospital, so I'll need to take at least a week off.

Discuss your plans, but don't be overly specific so you have flexibility. Besides, once you've made a promise, people will expect you to stick with it. So don't get boxed in.

Don't

- I will be back on Thursday morning.
- I can devote at least three hours a day to projects.

- I will call every morning promptly at 8:00 for the morning meeting.
- I will help _____ finish the _____.

Do

- I will be back sometime at the end of the week.
- I can devote at least an hour or two a day.
- I'll try to be in touch every morning. If I miss the morning meeting, Claire can forward me the notes.
- I will help _____ with the project.

Sometimes you won't need time off—just different hours. In this case, you really do need to be specific:

Don't

- I will work less time.
- I need to keep different hours.
- I will try to make my deadlines or figure out alternatives.
- For the foreseeable future, I will need to arrive late for work.

Do

- I will work 20 hours a week.
- I need to work from 10:00 to 6:00 for the next two weeks.
- I'll do my best to make deadlines or alert Claire, who can reassign them to someone else.
- For at least a month, I will need to arrive at work at 10:00.

It's always helpful to send an "if-then" message, so all those involved know what they can expect from you:

If . . .   then . . .

- If I am out on Tuesday, then I will make up the work at the end of the week.
- If I don't answer my phone, then try calling my cell.
- If you need to get into my e-mail account, then ask Sarah for my password.

Set boundaries on your availability:

- You can reach me in the early mornings and late afternoons.
- I will be able to complete the existing projects on schedule but can't take any new ones until I return.
- I will be able to work part-time hours only for the next few weeks.
- I will need to leave at 3:00 every afternoon.

Quick tip: Even though your coworkers seem sympathetic, don't treat them as confidantes, telling them about the miseries of your life. Instead, trust them with information that will explain your absence or altered work schedule, and save the personal details for conversations after work.

You Must Leave Your Job for Personal Reasons but May Want to Return Eventually

People leave their jobs for many reasons. They get burned out. Find better positions. Return to school. In these cases, they can simply say good-bye and wish everyone the best. But the plot shifts when you're leaving a job but might want to come back later. Your departure must be carefully planned: no sudden exits and dropped projects in your wake. And you must do a good enough job of explaining why you're leaving so no one feels insulted or stranded. These perfect phrases will keep the doors open, even when you close them.

Say What You Like About the Job

Be specific and sincere. Determine what you really did like about the job, and express it. Obviously, the specifics depend on your experience, but your openings may start like this:

- I really enjoyed . . .
- Thank you for giving me . . .
- What I most appreciated was . . .
- When I arrived I was . . . , but after a few weeks, I . . .
- The experience taught me that . . .
- My favorite aspect was . . .
- The best part for me was . . .
- I am proudest of . . .

Or the final statement may say something like this:

- I've really enjoyed working with all of you—the energy was so high and the demands were constant, but we still had fun!

- The opportunity to work on new systems was amazing—I think I learned more than I did in college.
- I am proudest of the way we handled the McCain account. Everything went so smoothly thanks to our great teamwork.
- I'm really going to miss those strategy sessions on Tuesday.

Just avoid insincere-sounding expressions like these:

- Thank you for your support.
- Thank you for the opportunities.
- I will always remember all of you.
- I derived a great deal of satisfaction from this job.

Remind them that you'd like the option to return:

- I hope that someday I can return and work with you again.
- Although I am taking on new challenges, I see all of you in my future, sooner than you might think!
- I'd love to return with my new insights and experiences to participate in the team again.

Explain Why You Need to Leave in Clear and Understandable Terms

Make sure you focus on the positive aspects of what's ahead and not the negative side of why you need to go.

Don't

- I'm not getting enough stimulation here and need to go back to school.
- I'm totally burned out by the pressure and long hours you require.

- I find the people impossible and want to escape.
- The pay structure and promotion opportunities are too small.

Do

- I want the stimulation that I can get by returning to school.
- I need to work fewer hours and have a chance to pace myself.
- I'd like to work for a smaller business or even work for myself.
- I'd like to work in an environment where I can grow into new and higher positions.

Be Precise About the Timing of Your Exit

- I plan to leave on ____. This will give us three weeks to prepare for my exit and for you to start finding a replacement.
- I will leave after we complete ____, which I expect will be in about two weeks.
- My plan is to transition out. I will go to part time from January through March. I plan to leave on April 1.
- Because I was unexpectedly accepted into the program, I must leave in two weeks. I will be available to discuss projects and pitch in on unfinished work for two weeks after that.

Ask What You Can Do to Make Your Departure Easier

- I plan to tie up any loose ends before I leave. If you have anything in particular that needs my attention, please let me know.

- Please let me know how I can help make my departure easier.
- If you need anything in particular from me before I go, just let me know. I will be cleared out of the office on _____. If you give me ample advance notice, I'll be sure to complete the job.
- I am going to complete as many of my assignments as possible. Since some weren't due for a few months, I'll organize them so my replacement can easily jump in. Is there anything else you want me to do?

Send Good-Bye Notes

Send individuals notes thanking people who helped you most or with whom you established strong working relationships. A hard-copy note is always nice: it's tangible and shows thought. However, an e-mail is better than nothing. You only need a line or two. They'll think well of you, should you return for a job. Be specific and sincere. The actual content depends on your experience, of course, but might look like this:

- Thanks so much for helping with those midnight proposals and for making me laugh with all those jokes I won't mention here!
- All that time you devoted to helping me manage the data system really helped. I'll take that learning with me no matter what I finally do.
- I wish you the best with the McCain project. I know, as usual, you'll do a great job.
- I'll really miss our lunches—hopefully, we'll connect now and then for a few more.

Part Five

In the Fire of Sabotage and Insubordination

Yes, work is hard enough. But having to address other people's ill will, from undercutting comments to unfulfilled tasks, only makes it harder. Yet, like many other communications in difficult situations, your response can have legal implications. You never know which ones may show up in court or your lawyer may use to get money that belongs to you. So you must remember several points when writing: consider them your defense, your strategy, and, above all, your legal armor should the worst occur:

- *Document everything.* Make sure you e-mail repeating every important communication, and save it for years to come. You never know when the problem will haunt you—even when it seems to be resolved. Talk on the phone? Have a meeting? Then follow up with an e-mail repeating the major points in your discussion.
- *Get witnesses.* Make sure that you have witnesses, particularly when discussing egregious behavior. You may want to mention the person in passing by saying something like: "In our meeting with Joel, you said . . ." Or keep your own records. Regardless, cc'ing someone, whether a boss, lawyer, or senior-level expert, always helps.
- *Use objective language.* Be sure that you use accurate and specific language—with no feelings involved. For example, avoid saying: "You insulted me in front of the group." This would meet a simple denial, as in: "No, I did not." Instead, be clear and say: "At the meeting on the 19th, you said that I was 'too stupid to think straight'" and other insulting

lines. If someone is raising his or her voice, try to add an objective quality by saying, for example: "Several customers asked Carl what the commotion was all about."

- *Be clear about what you want.* The reason you send a message about an inappropriate or counterproductive interaction is simply to inspire a response. But what should that response consist of? Do you want them to stop engaging in a certain behavior? Leave a project? Get fired? Or do you want them to pay a bill . . . with interest? Be clear about what you want in your own mind—then state it on the page. Otherwise, you're just letting off steam.

- *Never pose a threat you don't mean.* Very often, if you're angry or tired of dealing with a difficult situation (yet again), you might be tempted to threaten to call an attorney, report them to an association or consumer agency, or take some other action. Be sure not to threaten something you don't mean though; you may want to make them shiver with fear, but they might call their attorney instead.

A Constant Air of Passive-Aggressive Whining Undermines Team Morale and Energy

Passive-aggressive behavior, especially en masse, can be deadly. You don't know what to expect, how to strategize, or whom to trust. So your main mission is to take control, making tasks, professional relationships, and even behavior as clear and indisputable as possible.

When Passive-Aggressive Colleagues Sabotage You on a Project

Focus on the project—rather than on yourself—even when you think the passive-aggressive behavior is personal.

First: State the negative actions using objective and measurable language:

- We agreed that you would____ by Friday. Yet you didn't complete that task, nor did you notify me or anyone else on the team that you wouldn't.
- On the telephone at 9 a.m., you said that you would have ____ ready. When I arrived, though, you were unprepared.
- You told me that you would ____ for four hours a day. Yet the records indicate that you did not take these steps even once.
- In our project plan, you were supposed to ____ by ____. Yet now you claim you haven't even started on that task.

Then: Show how that affected the team:

- As a result, we will not be able to _____, as planned. This will create cash flow problems, as we cannot bill until you have completed these steps.

- I was unable to work with our client in a fast and effective manner. As a result, the customer was dissatisfied, as you know from her e-mail to the boss.
- We do not _____, as we agreed in our game plan. This sets us back by weeks, possibly months.
- Three of us will have to pitch in to stay on track.

Next: Discuss what you expect from the team:

- You must complete _____ *plus* _____ to make up for the delay. We will follow up on your progress in our Tuesday meetings.
- You must send the customer an apology note and offer to make up for the problem somehow. Please cc me and the boss on this.
- You must provide ___ by ____.
- You must get started immediately and send all of us on the team a running record.

When Colleagues' Gossip Undermines Your Reputation in the Office

Confront them directly, and state that you want that behavior to stop:

- I understand that you have plenty to say about the state of my personal life. This kind of attack is unprofessional, and you need to stop.
- According to several people in the office, you said that ____. This makes you look bad—as well as me—and you need to stop.
- Keep your comments about my personal life to yourself.
- If you have comments on my work style, say them to me.

Sometimes, passive-aggressive colleagues attempt to undermine your power by telling you the negative comments other people have told them about you. This is hurtful, unprofessional, and inappropriate, so tell them to stop:

- Please stop telling me that ___ doesn't like the way I dress. It doesn't have anything to do with work.

- You seem to be getting a lot of insights about what people think of me personally. This leads me to think you are gossiping about me—this is unprofessional, and you should stop.

- I really don't care what ___ or anyone else thinks about my ___, so don't bother to tell me.

When getting control of employees who undermine your authority through passive-aggressive behavior:

- Once we decide that ___, it's not negotiable or up for discussion.

- If you have issues about my management style, schedule a meeting, and we'll discuss them.

- I understand that many of you have had doubts about the project. It's counterproductive to discuss them among yourselves; we should have a meeting to discuss them together.

- If you have any questions about the project, bring them directly to me or one of the team leaders—we can give you an accurate response.

Follow the phrase with an objective example of how they undermined your authority.

When Addressing a Group of Employees Who Are Stuck in Whine Mode

- From now on, let's discuss what can happen, not what didn't.
- Let's write all your complaints in one column of the flip chart page and the solutions in the other.
- Why not break into groups and draw up a plan for how you will solve these problems?
- What do all of you think is a good approach?

If you don't get a spoken response, stop the meeting and suggest they write a few ideas down and then report in.

Associates Try to Steal Your Project

Maybe your associates think they're better qualified for the work. More entitled. Or that a loophole in a contract allows them to take it from you. No matter—if the project is yours and you worked hard on it, work equally hard to keep it with these perfect phrases.

When You Realize Someone Is Trying to Steal Your Project

State how you know what the person is up to and provide evidence that the project is yours. The order doesn't matter—just be sure that you are concrete and support your points:

- _____ told me that you were planning to _____ in the project. Our contract specifies that my company is responsible for this aspect of the job, as you can see in this paragraph: *(quote paragraph)*.
- I recently learned that you were _____. In my meeting on December 6, the client asked me to be responsible for this task, and we have begun that project already. I have e-mails which support this fact. I can send them if you like.
- According to our agreement, we are responsible for _____ through the summer of 2010. If you would like to add your employees to the project, contact me directly and we'll discuss whether we have a need.
- As we agreed in April 2007, you are a subcontractor to us. As a result, you cannot initiate any actions on this project without first consulting with us.

Alert the Client or Project Manager

Be friendly and matter-of-fact. You don't want to embroil your client in an angry interaction between you and the other party.

- Just to let you know, we have already begun to _____, as you requested on June 14. We just learned that _____ is undertaking similar steps; thought you'd like to know before we duplicate efforts.
- I spoke with ___ yesterday. Apparently, ___ is planning to _____. We already agreed to undertake that aspect of the project and have experts in place and will continue moving forward.
- As you know, we have a project plan in place and have already initiated the first two phases. _____ may have a plan of their own; switching gears partway into the project will be time consuming and expensive.

When helpful, get the client to support your side of the situation:

- As we discussed in the team meeting, you want us to _____ by _____. If this is not the case, let me know.
- According to our contract, my team is responsible for _____. _____ has told us that it is planning to take over this task. Could you clarify so we can continue moving ahead?
- Some questions have been coming up about who is responsible for _____. Could you please confirm?

Alert Your Colleagues or Staff to the Situation

- As you know, we have been providing ___ with _____ services for two years. This is in our contract. If you see that anyone is taking over these tasks, please let me know.

- We have been working as the lead on the ____ project, which we won through a competitive bid in 2003. Our contract is good for another two years. Should you receive instruction from anyone else, please notify me at once.
- According to an e-mail I received recently, ____ is planning to engage in the ____ that we have been working on. Yet ____ is not authorized to do so. If anything changes, please let me know.

Your Company or Business Partners Are Lying to the Client About the Scope of Work So They Get More Business

No question—not everyone is cut out to be a whistle-blower, especially when alerting a client about the client's own company. But you may not have to take such drastic steps. Just letting your colleagues know they're doing the wrong thing may be enough to stop them. Here are some perfect phrases that can help, without getting you in hot water.

When Providing Feedback About a Proposal

- This looks good, except for line 1. We've never needed that much time to ____. Why don't we cut down by two days?
- We can cut the time for our services in half if we eliminate ___ and ___. This won't affect the outcome, and the client will be happy with the rate.
- In our previous proposals, we only needed ____ amount of time for the ____. Unless there's a good reason, let's provide our standard arrangement.
- I think this proposal is really overpriced. We should aim for ___. That's only fair for the client.

When Discussing a Project at a Meeting

- I think we need to discuss the realistic costs under the "scope of work" section.
- Guys, we do really great work, but I'm concerned that we're overcharging the client.
- I understand that we're adding "padding" just in case. How about if we give them a price range and try to stay low?

- This proposal doesn't seem quite fair, as our rates have not gone up; yet this client would pay 25 percent more than everyone else.

When Determining How to Bill the Client That Week

Be straightforward, and focus your comments on individual expenses. Be sure to discuss individual dates and times. The specifics will depend on your situation, obviously, but may sound like this:

- We charged them for two business lunches on May 10 and 21. I attended both lunches, but we didn't discuss the client once.
- We only spent two hours, from 3:00 to 5:00, on the project on January 10.
- Let me know if you want me to review my notes, but I'm certain that Lonny didn't attend the May 1 debrief, so we can't bill them for his time.
- I invited our employees to meet with the client as a friendly gesture on December 30, but not as a work session. So we shouldn't bill them.

Service Providers Don't Supply What They Promised

Nowhere else is documentation as helpful as here. You must document every agreement, what they did or didn't provide, and evidence that this occurred. Write the occurrences down as they happen; then when e-mailing or talking to the provider, you should use your records as evidence to support your point.

When Pointing Out the Problem

- In my contract, you stated that you would provide____. I never received this service.
- You stated that you would provide ____ on ____. I received the service two days late, and it has been interrupted three times since.
- In my agreement, you said a ___ and ____ would be assigned to help me. Yet I have not heard from any of them.
- You said that___, who is in charge of my account, would help me ____ and ____. Yet ____ denies that these are his responsibilities.

When the Problem Persists

- When I signed on for the service, I agreed to pay $____ for the following: ____. I only received these services: (*list, with the dates you received them*) although you billed me for the complete package.
- As I stated in my e-mail of May 14, I still have not received ____. Also the ___ that you provided has the

following problems: ____. I contacted ____ about this several times the week of May 1 but have not seen an improvement.

▪ Since August 14, when I first signed on for your service, I have encountered the following problems: ____. I have documented each of these in detail and can send my notes if you like.

When You Get What You Requested but the Product or Service Is Bad

▪ The ____ that you sent me has the following problems: ____.

▪ While your employees have provided the services in your agreement, they did not respond to my calls on ___ and ____ and did not fix the ___ that was not working correctly from ___ to ___.

▪ I have consistently had problems with the services that you provide, particularly with the ___ and the ___. I have e-mailed you about these problems. I can send copies if you like.

▪ You did not provide the ___ or the ____, as stated in my contract. Further, the ____ had the following problems: _____. I outlined these in numerous e-mails as well as telephone conversations, all of which I have documented.

You Get Charged for Services You Didn't Want

▪ I have been receiving your ____ since ___ although I never requested it. Although I asked you to discontinue the service, you continue to provide it.

- Please stop sending me the ____. I never asked to receive it and do not intend to pay my bill.
- I just realized that you added ___ to my normal bill. You never informed us that we would have to pay extra for this service. Please discontinue the service and strike the expense from my monthly bill.
- My associate informed me that you have been billing us for ____ under the ____. Yet we never received this service, nor do we want it.

Quick tip: In some cases, you may want compensation for poor service. If so, how do you know what to request? And when to request it? My advice—let them make the move. Here's why: you may be asking for less than they're willing to give. In that case, you're stuck. If they offer less than you want, you can always demand more.

Here are a few perfect phrases when demanding compensation. *And remember:* Be fair and be tough!

- Please tell me how you will compensate me for these problems.
- What do you plan to do about these problems in the future?
- How will you make up the difference to me?
- I derailed my project goals because of these problems. How do you plan to address this?
- These problems have been costly: I can send you a breakdown of expenses I've incurred as a result. You need to compensate me for the difference.

There's a Sudden Exodus of Employees to Your Competitor

And they're . . . off. Employees, who loved you and your firm, run off to the competitor. How do you stop more from leaving? And how do you manage without them? And . . . how do you manage morale issues with the ones who are left? Perfect phrases are in order here. But first check your own morale, and remember, every chaotic event offers a chance to move ahead.

Create a Sense of Belonging to the Team

People are leaving, and everyone knows it. Rather than be in denial, why not discuss the event—even *leverage* it—to create a team that's stronger than before. Here are some ways to do that:

- Well, some folks have left, and we miss them. But this is a great chance to set a newer and stronger direction for all of us.
- Since we're a smaller staff now, we can really pull together and make things happen.
- We're in a great position to grow as a team and bring in new people who are sharp and energetic.
- We're the die-hard loyalists, and it's up to us to make sure our company continues to grow, and grow beyond the competitors.

Get Them to Take Ownership: Ask Their Opinions and Follow Through

Rely on positive language, and focus on what's ahead. Avoid dwelling on the negatives.

Don't

- If you have any problems, let me know.

- We don't want to lose you, so let us know what bothers you and we'll see what we can do.

- I know things have been tough around here and that's why people are leaving. So what can we do to become better than we are?

Do

- What are some ideas you have for making the company an even better place to work?

- As you know, we have a suggestion box. Please let us know your thoughts, and be sure to raise your ideas at meetings, too. We're open to hearing them.

- What would you like to see as the future of our company?

Infuse Them with a Sense of Purpose

- We plan to continue growing and giving back to the community as we do.

- As always, we want to maintain our reputation as a strong, profitable company that is ethical and fair.

- We'll continue treating ourselves and others with respect in all our interactions.

- We plan to forge ahead, finding new and exciting technologies that improve the lives of everyone.

- We plan to grow into the most innovative and successful company in our region.

Create Clear Goals and Objectives

Whatever the goals and objectives, underscore that you will achieve them by working as a team:

- We'll work together to double our profits within the next three years.
- Our objective is to open branch locations in the three districts. We'll work closely together and reward you for your success.
- Our single goal is to build our membership to record highs by the end of the year. We can do this through an aggressive and open working relationship.

Your Company Gets Bought Out in a Hostile Situation

So now your company is at the hands of what's tantamount to the enemy. But face it—you're still there. Your team's still there. And who knows, maybe you'll even like the new company. But the trick is to convince your coworkers and employees so they don't abandon you. These perfect phrases, and a little time, will help.

When Breaking the News

If you're a team leader or a manager, you may need to break the news to your employees. Better get there quickly, too, and beat the rumor mill and the media. Let them know about the buyout or takeover, being careful to frame it in the most realistic and positive sense.

- I just learned that _____ is now our parent company. I'm not expecting any elaborate changes, so let's keep focusing on what's ahead.

- _____ has just closed the deal. As I understand it, this might make the workplace better. The company has a history of investing heavily in its employees.

- Just so you know, we're now working for _____. Our mission and the great services will remain the same. In fact, it's possible the only thing that will change is our name and some of the senior-most managers.

Quick tip: Let employees feel confident that you'll keep them in the information loop. Be specific—let them know exactly how you'll do this. Remember, one of the major sources of anxiety for employees is feeling out of control. Regular updates can help them immeasurably:

- I'll update you about changes in our regular Monday meeting.
- If you hear gossip, don't believe it. Come to me immediately, and I'll tell you what's true and what isn't.
- I'll e-mail all of you regular updates about the merger as news comes in.
- I'll be attending the weekly manager's meeting. So plan to meet with me immediately after in the small conference room. I'll fill you in about any changes.

When Coworkers and Employees Express Anger or Concern

- You need to wait until you see what changes happen. So far, we have no idea.
- Changes like these are just part of business life. So do yourself a favor and don't worry about it. Just wait and see.
- This company is highly profitable and has more opportunities for growth. So this may be a good thing.

- It's hard to know what's ahead. But it's a solid company, and I'm optimistic.
- Change can feel hard, regardless of whether or not it's merited by reality. I think we all need to breathe deeply, relax, and wait to see what's ahead.

When Addressing Issues with HR Representatives

Aside from convincing others the company isn't going to the dark side, you may need to convince yourself. So ask the right questions and get concrete information. If the news is good—great! If the news is bad—you're still better off knowing it. Think hard, though, about what you really need to know. Here are some examples of questions you might ask:

- What can I expect from my health insurance plan?
- What is the company's retention history?
- What is its policy about promoting from within?
- What is its history regarding layoffs?
- How heavily does the company rely on contractors?
- What are its training programs like?
- Does the company have strong community and charitable programs? What are the company's policies regarding giving?

Remember, do not ask subjective questions. It's unlikely the HR representative will (or should) express his or her perspective from a personal point of view.

Don't Ask

- Do you like this company?
- Do you think it's trustworthy?

- When do you think it will start making life hard for us?
- So you think we have job security with this company?
- I really love my manager. Think he'll be on his way out?
- Is it the type of company that makes sudden, unpredictable changes?

When Meeting New Leadership

This is your chance to ask questions about vision, timing, and policy issues the HR representative couldn't address. Come fueled with facts that help frame your question and enable the new leaders to give you clear and helpful answers.

- When you took over _____ Company, you closed the customer care unit and outsourced it abroad. Do you have plans to do this here?
- What are your goals for the company in concrete terms? For example, do you plan to continue expanding?
- What are some of the culture differences between our two companies, and what can we expect?

Part Six

Pressure Cookers

D eadlines missed, looming, and unexpected are simply a part of business life. Some people thrive on them; most people don't. Regardless, they require energy and clear thinking, and your messages must reflect and inspire this. That means you must throw away long, dragging sentences, tired phrases, and thick, boring paragraphs that reflect a certain slowness that the recipient will ignore. Instead, keep your message fast and exciting, inspiring people to move, move, move. Here are some tips about how:

- *Use short sentences.* These give the recipient a sense of speed, mission, and importance. Pretend, for a minute, that you see smoke pouring out of a window in your office. Which would you be more inclined to say:
  - If you look out the window of the seventh floor, you know, where the cafeteria is located, you'll notice thick, white smoke and lots of it. My assumption is that there's a fire there. I'm not certain about why the alarm hasn't sounded, but it would be preferable if we all got out.
  - Look! Fire on the seventh floor. Smoke's pouring out the window. Right where the cafeteria is. Why isn't the alarm sounding? Come on; we better get out.

Naturally, you'd say the second option. So don't articulate urgent or timely matters as if you had all day. The recipient will act in kind.

- *Avoid dense language.* This is *not* the time to use industry language or, worse, jargon. They simply create a slow feel.

Instead, energize your message with sharp verbs, short, tight phrases, and accessible words. In short, if you wouldn't use these words in daily conversation, then you shouldn't use them here.

- *Be direct.* Tell your recipients exactly what they need to do. Don't be suggestive or leading. Get to the point. Notice the difference:
  - It's really important that you get the content to me in a timely fashion—end of day at the latest. This will enable me to get it to Charlie on time.
  - Get the content to me by 5:00. I'll review it and send it to Charlie.
- *Watch those subject lines.* If you're sending e-mails, make sure you keep the subject lines peppy. Every word must be energy-charged and reflect that the message within is timely.

More ideas and plenty of perfect phrases wait ahead.

Tight Deadline for a Project

What you want is clear—get the recipient to take an action and drop everything else that he or she is doing. So, yes, keep it fast, clear, and clean. In these situations, it's best to call *and* e-mail. You never know which will reach the person soonest. If you do connect by phone first, send a follow-up e-mail, including tasks and timing, to avoid any confusion.

Subject Line on an E-Mail

Make it fast—a few explosive words at most.

Don't

- The XYZ form due today
- Project requirement for today
- Implementation plan needed by IT
- Budget deadline was yesterday

Do

- Send travel form now!
- Project deadline 2:00
- Slam deadline on plan!
- Need budget

You can use humor or irony to give your subject line some pizzazz. How far you go obviously depends on your company, the person receiving the e-mail, and the seriousness of the matter. Here are a few examples.

Serious and Effective

- Send travel form now!

Humorous and Effective

- Today: Send form or stay home
- The plane isn't leaving

Serious and Effective

- Need budget now!

Humorous and Effective

- Send it or lose it by 3:00
- Need money? Better hurry!
- Budget bank is closing!

> *Quick tip*: If you have a choice, use the most relaxed language—even with names. Say your budget form is titled B08–262 for reasons only your company knows. Rather than say "B08–262 Due," which will get lost in the typical sea of subject lines wavering in everyone's box, use plain language: "Budget form due now!" Then you can use the form in the body of the text.
>
> When possible, give the recipients a caveat. You must be honest—don't invent, even though it's tempting:
>
> - Two spaces left for training!
> - Send budget today or no funding
> - Health plan options close at 5:00

Body of an E-mail

Elaborate on the message in your subject line. But remember, you *still* don't have the luxury of using long, drawn-out sentences or chatty introductions. So avoid openers like these.

Don't

- At my meeting with the project lead earlier today, I learned that our deadline, originally scheduled for Friday, has been bumped up to this afternoon.
- I wanted to remind you that you need to get me the acquisition form by 4:00 today or you will not be able to make purchases until February.
- I heard from a client about the new product. He says that our contract states we would send ___ by May 1—two weeks ago. Unless we send it immediately, he will contact his lawyer. I checked his contract, and he does, indeed, have a case.

Do

- Important: our Friday deadline is now this afternoon. Get me everything by 4:00!
- You cannot make purchases until February if you don't send the acquisition form by 4:00 today.
- We must get the client a new ___ today, or he will contact his lawyer. Note: we're late, and he does have a case.

What to Say in a Phone Call

As in an e-mail, don't warm up with a friendly hello or a sentence like "You gotta minute?" Instead, get right to the point.

The specifics depend on your situation, of course, but would sound something like this:

- We have an urgent deadline on our hands.
- The deadline for the McCain client is bumped. You must get me everything by 4:00.
- Charlie just called. We have to get Accounting our budget by 3:00, or the project is off.
- If you want to be reimbursed for the trip, get Beth your expenses before lunch. If not, you won't see a dime until February.

Sudden Deadline Because of Unexpected Problems

When problems pop up, you must alert people without causing them to panic, get angry, or have other strong negative reactions. Instead, get them to take action by focusing on a solution.

When the Client Will Be Affected

Quickly explain what happened and how the client will be affected *even if* the recipient knows this:

- ____ just alerted us to the fact that ___ and ___ aren't working. We need to repair this immediately, or ____ could occur.
- The ____ that we put in ____'s office has collapsed. Contact the contractor—I'll head to the client's right now.
- The ____ broke. Please fix this right away, and I'll follow up with the client.
- The ___ we promised the client last week still isn't ready. We must get on this right away.

Use strong, excited verbs, not weak ones:

Replace	With
told	alert
said	announced
isn't working	broke/died/stopped

When You Detect a Security Breach

Tell people what happened and what they should do. Don't speculate about the grim possibilities or dwell on the reasons why they must act quickly.

- Important: the system detected _____. This could affect everyone in our building.
- Security breach detected on _____. Shut down the building immediately.
- Three visitors without security tags were spotted in our building. Send officers to investigate, please. Last seen in lobby.
- The security door was propped open on my floor. I just called security—better check your doors.

When Someone on Your Team Made a Big (and Stupid) Mistake

When Speaking to the Person

- The _____ that you developed for the client stopped working. You must correct this immediately; or the ___ and ___ will be affected.
- You accidentally gave the client _____. Get him the correct ___ right away, and send a follow-up notice to his manager.
- We agreed that you would ____. Yet you neglected to do this, and now the ____ is ____. You need to take these steps immediately: _____.

Quick tip: When contacting someone else for support, you may want to discuss who was responsible for the mistake, or you may want to be discreet and not name anyone. This depends on several factors: the dynamics of the situation, how large a role that person played in the outcome, and how much the recipient knows about the task involved.

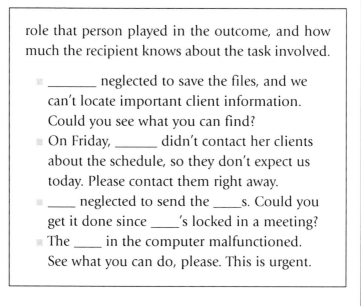

- _____ neglected to save the files, and we can't locate important client information. Could you see what you can find?
- On Friday, _____ didn't contact her clients about the schedule, so they don't expect us today. Please contact them right away.
- ____ neglected to send the ____s. Could you get it done since ____'s locked in a meeting?
- The ____ in the computer malfunctioned. See what you can do, please. This is urgent.

Quick tip: Regardless of whether you're in a crisis, you're solving problems, or you're under a deadline, be precise. Let the recipients know exactly what happened, what they need to do, and when they need to do it. By the way—try not to give too much lead time. This can work against you, since people will forget. If you do, be sure to follow up as the time draws near.

Don't

- As soon as possible (when is that?)
- At your earliest convenience (it's never convenient)
- Whenever you can (that's just about never)

Do

- Immediately
- Within the hour
- By 5:00 today

Tight Deadline Because a Competitor Threatens to Launch a Product—or Open a New Business—Before You Do

Actually, this is the easiest deadline message to convey. It gives you an external force that pushes employees to action. It sets up a healthy, competitive racelike feeling, full of energy and *charge*. And it lets you know when you've won the race or didn't. Here are the phrases that push you out the starting gate.

When You Just Heard the News

Generally, you should follow this structure:

What you heard . . . What you must do to compete

- We just heard that ____. Let's see if we can get ____ going next week.
- ____ is going to introduce its new ____ early this summer. Let's get cranking and introduce ours on ___.
- ____ is planning to move into the ____. We better increase our presence there immediately. Let's get on the phone with PR.
- Just learned that ____ is about to ____. Let's contact advertising. We need a more aggressive campaign.

Here are some specific examples of how it might look:

- Just heard that Marshall's is going to open a new store in Boston this summer. We better hustle to finalize our agreement with the real estate developers so we can have our doors open in spring.

- RDIR is going to launch its new program in two weeks. Tell PR to get some press releases out so we can make a big splash right away.
- Just heard on the wire that EveryTech plans to put out a new version of its software. Are we ready to launch? See if R&D can speed up the pace.

When Your Team Is Moving Too Slowly

You can use the "If we don't, then . . ." strategy:

If we don't . . .   **then . . .**

- If we don't finish _____ by May, then ____ will be on the market first.
- If we don't find an office soon, then _____ will tap into our market.
- If we don't finish developing the product, then we may be too late getting it on the shelves.
- If we don't get aggressive with our campaign, then we'll be buried by their advertising.

Or you can use an advantage-first approach, saying, "So we can . . ., we must . . ."

So we can . . . ,   **we must . . .**

- So we can get media attention, we must announce the product first.
- So we can get people to sign up, we must launch a door-to-door campaign next month.
- So we can get people to sign up with us, we must canvass the shopping malls before the holiday season.

Let the content determine which works to your advantage the most.

You Derail a Project and Must Explain to the Customer

Talk about grace under fire. You derailed the project, and the one who's most affected is your client. So you must show concern but not panic. Be apologetic but not humiliated. Act quickly without breaking into chaos. Phew. Now what? Follow up, to make sure your client forgives you and wants to move on.

Letting the Client Know

This requires strategy . . .

If . . . the problem is relatively easy to fix, say what you need to do, then why.

- We'll need to reinstall the ____ to get your ____ working again.
- We need to replace the _____, which should only take an hour, since the original burned out.
- We need to ____. This is simple to do, and your ____ should be up and running within an hour.

If . . . the problem will take time to fix, say what happened and how you can fix it:

- The _____ was not secure, so it slipped out of place. As a result, we will need to ____.
- Because the ad copy had several misspellings, we will need to redesign and print it again. This will take two additional weeks.
- We found that the ____ was the wrong size. We will need to construct and implement a new one.

When possible, show the advantage of your taking great care in repeating the steps. If possible, highlight the advantages:

- This will ensure that _____.
- As a result, the _____ will be even better than before we began.
- In the process, we will look for any _____.
- We will try to identify any _____ also, which will help you _____ in the future.
- As we go, we will note any _____ and get you that information. It will help you . . .

Avoid overly negative language. The situation is bleak; no need to make it bleaker.

Don't

- Unfortunately, you will not be able to_____ until we make these repairs.
- We were unable to _____.
- We cannot use the one we have now.
- You cannot begin until _____.

Do

- You will be able to_____ once we make these repairs.
- We still need to _____.
- We need to give you new ones.
- You can begin on _____.

When Offering Something Extra as Compensation

You should do this first when you contact them and later when you follow up. Generally, you will use phrases like these:

- To make up for the delay, we will . . .
- Of course, we will not bill you for . . .
- We will add an extra _____ to your contract.
- In addition to the _____, we will send you a _____ as an apology.
- The _____ and the _____ normally cost $_____. But we will only charge you _____ to cover the manufacturer's expense.

When Following Up on a Project You Derailed

No need to remind them of the problem—or apologize yet again. Instead, let them know what they're getting and that you promised it:

- As promised on _____, I am sending _____.
- Please note that we did not charge you for ___ or ___.
- In April, we said we would add another month to your contract without a fee. So we will continue your service without charge.
- You'll notice on line 5 of the invoice that we deducted _____ percent from your bill.

Because of New Requirements (Legal or Otherwise), You Must Redirect Your Employees, Your Paperwork, and Your Processes

Rules and regulations are hard enough for employees to abide by. Deviate, and a lawsuit may be pending. So you need to implement some quick project management strategies when new rules, regulations, and policy spring up. Why is this so hard? For one thing, people follow rules by habit. They do what they've always done. Now, suddenly, they have to change, which requires extra thought and energy and a certain amount of back stepping. So you need to make them snap to attention. Then, depending on the changes, you have morale to think about. Employees who are overworked have little patience for changes and may get discouraged.

Think of these perfect phrases as pick-me-ups that get them to pay attention and keep their spirits high as they do.

When Introducing New Rules and Regulations

Let them know who originated the changes—especially when your company has no involvement in them:

- The Department of _____ established these new regulations this fall.
- Because of changes to the ____, we must change our policies about ____.
- The ___ issued new guidelines for us to follow. I'm passing out copies for you to read.

The requirements for all ___ have changed as of the 1st according to the _____. From now on, you must do the following: _____.

When Addressing Concerns

Show how you'll support them—be specific, even if you don't have precise times:

- We'll be holding seminars to teach you how to manage the new requirements. I don't know the dates yet, but will get back to you soon.
- The company has produced a manual that addresses your questions.
- You can take an online training session any time—even from your house.

Reassure people by letting them know help is available. Be specific, giving contact names, e-mail addresses, phone numbers, and, when necessary, the time they'll be available:

- You can contact ___ in the HR Department with questions any time from 8:00 to 5:00 at ext. ___.
- The Help Desk is fully prepared to answer your questions. You can call or e-mail the people there any time during the workweek.
- E-mail me if you are confused about what to do—or stop by my desk. As long as the door is open, come on in.

When Addressing Anger or Other Forms of Push-Back

- I know this seems difficult, but you'll get used to it soon.
- This will become habit in no time.

- Just relax—when we introduced the old procedures, everyone thought they were complex, and now they seem easy. The same will happen for you.

Questions You Should Ask Others if Uncertain About New Rules and Regulations

- What should I do if _____ occurs?
- How does this affect situations like ____ and ____?
- What was the reason why they changed the existing procedures?
- Whom should I talk to if I'm uncertain about legal ramifications?
- What kind of training will the company offer?
- Does everyone in the company have to follow these policies or just our department?
- How do we know if we're doing them wrong?

Make sure that you know how to address your customers' concerns by asking these questions:

- Do our clients know about the changes?
- What should we tell them if they ask why the procedures are different?
- Whom should we send the customers to if they have questions about these changes?
- What if our customers insist that we follow the previous steps?
- Do you have any information printed out that we can give them?

Part Seven

Difficult Financial Situations

When addressing financial matters, be aware that for everyone—but especially those in business—finance is about more than numbers. It's about success, reputation, the future, and the payback of the past. Not to mention, ego, competitiveness, lifestyle, and a general sense of doing well—or not—in the world. Mess with people's finances and you've messed with a lot!

So if you find yourself engaged in a financial entanglement, remember that beneath your feet lie beds of hot, white coals. You need to settle your dispute without jeopardizing your relationship, and leave that difficult situation with a sense that the one ahead will be brighter and clear.

So when discussing financial matters, remember these perfect pointers:

- *Be objective.* Rely on unambiguous numbers backed up in paper by an agreement, a contract, or a written document. Of course, that assumes all your interactions are based on concrete and legal written documents, but that's for another book.
- *Discard emotion.* Put aside any emotions—whether you're angry, hurt, insulted, frustrated, or disgusted. And limit your discussion of what is or isn't fair. Instead, focus on actions: You agreed to pay a certain amount. They promised to give something concrete back in return. You promised and provided a service. They agreed to pay for it by a specific date.

■ *Keep a forward-looking approach.* Remember, you want to figure out a solution, not win a battle. So your communications must be focused on getting a result, not winning a competition or making a point.

Should they really want to rip you off (well, it does happen), then better pick up the phone and get some legal backing before you send another message.

Your Team Went Over Budget, and You Must Explain Why

This really is a problem. You agreed to do a certain amount of work and, experts that you are, gauged exactly how much it would cost for time and materials. Even better, you promised to squeeze out the value of every dollar. Then . . . guess what? Something happened; things changed. Better pull out these perfect phrases.

When Circumstances Beyond Your Control Caused the Problem

Be specific about the factors that affected your budget. The actual word use, of course, depends on your situation, but would look something like this:

- Because the cost of parts went up by 20 percent from the time we first drafted the budget, we need more money.
- We had to pay higher legal expenses than we anticipated because the _____ required additional costs.
- Because of the _____slump, we lost money in our initial round of investments.
- The figures that we received from the bank were off by 15 percent. This affected the budget we originally drafted.

When a Mistake on Your Team's Part Caused the Problem

Confess—clearly and in the most objective terms. Here are some opening phrases:

- We underestimated the costs of . . .
- We used last year's costs to determine this year's budget.

- We underestimated the amount of time it would take the contractors to complete that phase of the project.
- We overestimated their ability to complete that phase of the project with limited resources.

When the Other Party Has Options to Contain the Costs

- You have numerous options that can help contain the costs. Let me outline them for you.
- We can take different directions depending on the outcome and the timing you have in mind.
- We don't want to cut corners, but we can strategize ways of limiting the costs.
- I know a few ways you can cut additional costs and still have the outcomes you intended.

When It's Critical That They Don't Scrimp on Spending

You can acknowledge their perspective and then say why they shouldn't take financial shortcuts:

- I understand that you'd rather not invest more on this project, but the result could be that . . .
- I'm sure that ___ more money seems like a lot, but ultimately you'll spend much more money if you don't make the investment now.
- The budget made a lot of sense when we first discussed it. But for the reasons we discussed, you must add to it, or the ____ could be a loss.

Or get directly to the point:

- You need to invest ___ more dollars if you want the project to ultimately bring in a profit.

- The right parts cost 25 percent more than what you want to spend, but frankly, I wouldn't take the gamble.
- The only way we can complete the project is if you add $25,000 to your budget.

You Need Unexpected Funding

There are lots of possibilities for getting emergency funding, mainly because businesses large and small are so frequently in need. Whom you get your money from and why will dictate the content of your message. Of course, if you're getting a business loan, what matters most is your assets. But one way or another, you'll probably need these perfect phrases.

When You're under a Time Crunch and Need a Quick Financial Infusion

- In order to _____, we need $ _____ by the first of the month.
- We are short $____ and need to _____ by the 15th of the month.
- We were under by ___percent this quarter and need to make up the difference, or we won't be able to keep up with expenses.
- The only way we can overcome this setback is to get a quick infusion of $_____.
- If we get $____ by May 1, we will be able to make our payments.

When You Discover an Opportunity You Must Seize and Need the Capital to Do So

- The opportunity for growth is amazing, but only if we get $____ within the next two weeks.
- We have a really narrow window to cinch the deal and need $____ to do it. Our drop-dead deadline is _____.

- This is a remarkable opportunity, and the gains are undeniable. But we need to raise $_____ to achieve it.
- If we can raise $_____ within the next month, we can participate in this project. The returns potential is highly positive.

When Another Company or Business Is Challenging Your Business

- We need to raise $_____ immediately to offset the potential damage _____ can cause to our company through their new negative advertising campaign.
- We need to invest $ _____ into our _____, as _____ threatens to develop an exclusive patent.
- We need at least $_____ to ramp up our employee base and effectively compete with _____ for the multimillion-dollar project.

When Changes in the Market Require That You Invest in New Processes or Materials

State how much you need and the forces that require you get it:

- We need to update our ___ to keep up with technology changes in the _____. This will require an infusion of funding of approximately $_____.
- The market is now demanding _____. This will cost us approximately $___ to get our R&D efforts to the next step.
- With $_____ of seed money, we will be able to develop a ___ that more than meets market need.

When a Devastating Event Forces You to Seek Financial Backing

■ We lost our labs in the recent hurricane. We will need $____ to repair the damages and buy new equipment.

■ Owing to the fire last year, we needed to close our factories. To reopen them, and employ as many of our 200 employees who are still available, we will need $_____.

■ Because of the recession, consumer spending on ____ like ours has sunk beyond anyone's expectations. We need additional funding to develop the ___ component of our business.

You Learn Some of the Employees Are Stealing from the Company

This situation stinks no matter how you look at it. You need to stop the action simply because it's wrong. Yet you cannot incriminate yourself—even by association. Nor should you leave yourself vulnerable to attack should the culprit want revenge. Besides, do you really know who the thief is? Perhaps more than one employee is in on it. But don't worry. These perfect phrases will help you play the good guy, save your company money, and come up on top—where you belong.

When You're Unsure Who Is Stealing

You're concerned. Sure, you want to know who the culprit is. But more, you want the stealing to end. These phrases should help that happen.

In a Meeting

- I have come to realize that ___ has been missing from the company for several months, maybe longer. I don't want to blame any one person, but clearly someone here has been stealing.
- We have been short at least ___ every week after closing. I want all of you to be aware of how much money comes and goes from the register, as someone is quite clearly stealing.
- We need to discuss an important but difficult matter: someone is stealing from the company. Here's how I know . . .

In an E-Mail

- Please be aware that _____ has been missing from the company. Since this problem has been reoccurring for months now, we can only assume that someone is stealing.
- We are aware that someone has been taking the ___. You need to stop this behavior at once. Eventually you will get caught, and the situation will be difficult for all of us.
- If any of you knows how our _____ has vanished, please let me, or someone in security, know. Whatever you say will be kept confidential.

> *Quick tip*: Sometimes otherwise honest people find themselves stealing at work. They justify the action, telling themselves the company has more than enough supplies, or they're underpaid so why not steal a little something to make up the difference. Getting them to stop—especially when you don't know exactly who they are—can be as simple as bringing the crime to everyone's attention. Then an element of shame, and decency, will creep in.

When You Know Who Is Stealing and Confront Him or Her Directly

Be careful here. If you're wrong, you will create a seriously injurious situation and ruin a relationship beyond measure.

If you're right, and you need to be dead certain, then you should be clear about the outcome you expect. A confession? Unlikely. A denial? Probably. But at least the person will know he or she is being watched. So unless you've caught the person red-handed, an indirect approach may be the best one possible:

- I've noticed that money has been missing from the ____. Would you know where it went?
- Yesterday, I saw you put ___ in your bag. If I am mistaken, I apologize, but I did want to point out that is stealing.
- I overheard you tell ____ that you took ____. This is stealing, as I'm sure you know. And at this point, ___ is equally to blame for not turning you in.

When You Know Who Is Stealing and Need to Tell Your Boss

Be clear that you are not comfortable being a snitch and have nothing against the employee personally. But you couldn't let the thefts continue with a clear conscience.

- I feel uncomfortable bringing this up, but . . .
- As you know, ____ and I have gotten along quite well, so what I'm about to say is not personal.
- ____ is a really good employee in many ways. But I recently witnessed him . . .
- I really debated whether or not I should tell you this, but I know it's the right thing to do.
- I need to tell you something that is important but difficult to discuss . . .

Quick tip: Get your facts straight—this is no time for speculation. Then be as clear and accurate as possible. *Remember:* If you *think* you saw something but aren't sure—wait. Even a suggestion of wrongdoing could hurt that person's reputation.

Do Not Speculate

- I believe I saw her . . .
- It looked to me as though he . . .
- I noticed that she was glancing around after passing the cash register.
- It strikes me that he is the type to do that.
- I heard she has been in trouble before.

Do Be Definitive

- I saw her take the cash and put it in her pocket.
- The supply cabinet has been low lately, and he is the only one with a key to it.
- She admitted to me that she takes the supplies and resells them.

When Employees Discuss the Items They Steal in Front of You

- I think that's a bad idea: it's immoral and illegal, and you should stop immediately.

- Some people may think that's okay, but I don't. I think you should stop at the least and reimburse the business at best.
- I know you don't think there's anything wrong with stealing in this situation—but stealing is stealing, and it's wrong.

When Employees or Contractors Brag About Overcharging

- You should only be charging the amount you agreed to in your contract.
- Lots of contractors overcharge, but it's still wrong, and you need to stop.
- Either you start billing correctly, or I'll do something about it.
- What you're doing is wrong and illegal. Those of you who know about it and don't say anything are equally to blame.

You Can't Sell to a Favored Client Because His Back Payments Are Long Overdue

Yes, at one time this client was great: regular, agreeable, and quick with the payments. But he or she has fallen into hard times, and the unpaid bill for your services has grown depressingly long. You hate to do it, but you need to cut the client off. But the situation is more complex. Your client's luck will probably shift, and you don't want to lose him or her for good. Besides, you don't want to hurt the client's reputation—even within your organization. You just have an allegiance, and you can't let go. So what do you do? Trust these perfect phrases to help.

When Letting Your Client Know You Must Cut Him or Her Off

Where possible, explain that cutting him or her off is a business decision—nothing personal:

- As you know, you're one of my favorite clients. But company policy states that we can't provide services to customers with outstanding bills.
- I wish I could continue to be your ____. But you need to pay off the amount you owe. I'm sorry.
- Over the years, you've been a steady and agreeable client. If it were up to me, I'd continue providing services. But our Financial Department won't let me make exceptions to our policy.

If you've gone out of your way and have, say, stretched the rules, make sure your client knows. This may help to secure a bond once the client's fortunes have changed.

- Normally, we need to cut clients off after they've missed two payments. In your case, as you know, we far exceeded that.
- The company requires us to contact our Legal Department should customers delay paying their bill for over a month. In your case, I'm willing to wait.

When Trying to Make a Deal

- If you like, you can pay small amounts over a few months until the whole bill is paid off.
- I'd be willing to deduct 15 percent from your bill if that will help you pay it off.

When possible, get them to take responsibility, and find a reasonable arrangement that will work for them:

- What kind of payment schedule would work for you?
- When do you think you'll be able to pay your bill?
- Would you like to suggest a payment plan?

When Speaking with Internal People About the Client

You can't continue providing services, and your coworkers should know this. But you don't want to brand the client forever. So you need to be honest but discreet. So when coworkers ask whether the project will continue or why it's stopped, use these perfect phrases:

- They're not in a position to continue right now.
- They need to take a break from the _____. They'll let us know when they're ready to start again.
- They got hit by the _____ pretty hard and need to pull back on the services they're receiving.

- They're changing course for a while and focusing on other efforts.

When Speaking with Your Billing Department

- We need to adjust their billing cycle.
- Perhaps we could work something out with them regarding bills.
- Could you speak to them about their bills? We may need to work something out so they can pay us.
- Do you think we could create a payment plan so they can eliminate their debt to us?

You Have to Delay Your Employees' and Contractors' Pay Because of Cash Flow Problems

You have numerous issues to address in this type of communication. Obviously, your best bet is to ensure you're not in this difficult position in the first place. But as the cliché goes, these things happen. So you need to assure the employees that you're not the bad guy and will, indeed, pay up. And you must sustain their confidence by working up a plan where you pay them the back amount and continue with your payments moving forward. Finally, you must project a message that you are strong and in control, so they have confidence in your company, your mission, and your vision.

Letting the Employees Know That Paychecks Will Be Delayed

It's okay to express personal regret about having to delay paychecks. You feel bad about this and want the employees to know it.

First let them know the bad news:

- Unfortunately, I won't be able to pay you the full amount this week.
- Because of cash flow problems, I have to limit your paychecks. I wish I could pay you the full amount, but right now I can't.
- I'm sorry to say that I can only pay you half of your normal check this cycle.

Then tell them what you will do for them:

- I will pay you _____ this week and the full amount the next pay cycle.
- I will make up the difference in three installments on ___, ___, and _____.
- I do not foresee any problems ahead and will have paid off the full amount on ___.
- I developed this payment plan so you know what to expect moving ahead.

Explaining Why the Situation Happened

When they're blameless, the specifics will depend on your situation, but should look like this:

- As you know, we lost our biggest client recently. So our cash flow is pretty low right now.
- Since our expenses have skyrocketed, we have had trouble keeping up with our usual responsibilities.
- Because of the market shift, we have fewer clients than before.
- Our clients are considerably overdue in their payments to us.

When something they did created the situation:

- Because you did not bill me for two months, although I kept following up, I cannot pay you the full amount right now.
- As a result of having to revise your report for the client— and several other glitches—we are not getting our own payments in on time.

- Because the client went with another vendor after the ____ malfunctioned, we don't have the cash flow, as before.

Project a Sense of Moving Forward

True, you shouldn't promise anything you can't deliver or commit to anything you can't predict for certain. But be as optimistic and forward-looking as possible.

Don't

- We're getting money in by the end of the week.
- We're definitely going to win some great contracts this month.
- I'm looking forward to some big wins on the ____ and ____.
- I just know ____ will tell us to get started on that account.

Do

- I'm hopeful that we'll win several big contracts this month.
- Most likely, we'll get several checks in by the end of the month.
- We're working hard to win the ____ and ____ accounts: I can't imagine who would be better.
- We have some solid proposals out there now.
- Everyone's working hard and has great spirits; the money should start flowing in!

This situation can create less than perfect dynamics. You need to ask a business associate, even worse, a *client*, to do you a personal favor. At the same time, you don't want your client to see you as weak or vulnerable. Yet you really need the money and want the person to know how much you'll appreciate his or her efforts. These perfect phrases, and the dos and don'ts, should prove helpful.

When Asking for an Advance Partial or Full Payment

When you have a positive track record:

- Would you be able to pay 25 percent of the estimate up front? This would help us with some cash flow issues. As you know, we've always provided great service in the 10 years we've been doing business.
- As always, we'll provide the same ___ as we always have. Only, this time I was hoping you could pay some or all of the expense up front.

Note: You don't have to tell the client that you're having cash flow issues. Most likely, he or she will understand. When helpful, remind the client of an agreement that will guarantee you'll provide the product or service:

- As always, we'll abide by the stipulations in our contract.
- We will provide you with the precise services within the time frame in our project plan.
- As our letter of agreement states, you will receive ___ on ___.

Do *not* promise the client an extra service or better timing for up-front payment. This will seem like bribery. Besides, why shouldn't the client get that special deal every time, regardless?

When you have up-front expenses:

- I was hoping you could pay 25 percent to cover the ___ expenses. We usually don't ask you, but this time, we would appreciate the effort.
- Could you send us $____ to cover the ___ and ____? This will help us tremendously.
- Since your project requires a considerable amount of up-front costs, we were hoping you could send us $____ right away.

When Asking for a Payment within Days of Billing

- We just billed you for the ___ and ____ that we provided on ____. Could you possibly pay us early?
- I know that you usually have a 60-day turnaround for checks. But do you think you could pay us on ____, which is within 30 days, this time?
- Would you be able to pay the recent bill, number ____, dated ____, early this time?
- If possible, could you pay bill number ____ relatively soon? I'd be most appreciative.

> *Quick tip*: If you have a strong, personal relationship with a client, it's okay to say things like "I was hoping you could do me a favor and . . ." Or let

the client know that you're a bit squeezed this month. Still, if your situation feels dire, keep that to yourself and avoid terms like "terrible situation" or "dire problems."

When Asking for Payment of a Bill That's Overdue

Be specific so the client knows exactly which bill you mean and when you were expecting it to be paid:

- Could you please send us a check for bill number ____ regarding the ____ services we provided on ___. It was due on ____.
- Please let us know when we will receive a check for the ___ services that we provided on ___. We expected the payment on ____ but never received it.
- We sent a bill for the ____ that you received on ____. At that time, you agreed to pay us on ___, but we haven't received a check. When do you think you'll send it?

Quick tip: By the way, even if you're annoyed with a late check, watch your tone. A payment that's a week or two late could be an oversight or the result of cash flow or budget issues. Certainly, you don't want to alienate a perfectly good client and lose the good business that lies ahead.

You Can't Make Ends Meet on Your Current Salary and Need to Push Hard for a Raise

Your employer isn't your friend, nor is he or she in any way obliged to bail you out when times are tough. So you need to take a purely professional and businesslike approach when trying to get a raise. Your first step is to ask yourself these questions:

- Do I really deserve a raise?
- Are other people in my position getting more money than I am getting?
- Does company policy support the timeliness of my getting a raise? (For example, if you've only been working at the company for a short period, it won't even consider the request.)

If the answer to all three of these questions is yes, then ask yourself *these* follow-up questions. The answers will feed the perfect phrases you use when asking for that bump-up in your salary:

- What are the three most important reasons why I should get a raise?
- How much more are other people in my position getting?
- If I'm pretty much at the status quo, how do my activities benefit the company's bottom line—which will entitle me to an increase?

Then go ahead and confront your boss. Depending on your situation, you might want to e-mail him or her. But it's always best to sit down and discuss in a meeting. Don't just knock on the door and sit down in your boss' office, though. Set a time so he or she can really listen to your case and respond to it.

When E-Mailing for a One-on-One Meeting

Let your boss know the meeting will be short and positive:

- Could we have a short meeting, 15 or 20 minutes at most, where we could discuss my contributions to the company?
- I would like to meet with you next week. May I stop by on Monday morning?
- I'd like to talk with you about my role in the company. I'll contact _____ to see about scheduling a short meeting over the next few days.

When Asking for a Raise

Don't be pushy. Let your boss know that you value his or her role as a decision maker.

Don't

- I think I deserve a raise.
- I believe I am a hard worker and it's time for me to have a raise.
- I'd like to get more money for the work I'm doing here.
- I'm a good employee, and people compliment me all the time. So I think I am entitled to a raise.

Do

- I wonder if you would consider giving me a raise.
- I wanted to discuss my contributions with the hope that you'll consider giving me a raise.

I was hoping the company would increase my pay because of the results I've been able to achieve over the last six months.

Provide Evidence

You *must* be specific. If you think you're a hard worker, why should your boss or manager care? Does the customer agree? Has your hard work brought results, or are you busily creating useless activity? Don't expect your boss to know any of this; you must remind him or her.

Don't

- I'm a really hard worker.
- The clients love me.
- I always try to do a good job; if anything, I'm a perfectionist.
- I am unusually qualified for the job.

Do

- I usually arrive at 8:00 and leave at 5:00.
- Client ratings about my service have been high: in fact, 95 percent gave me a score of "excellent."
- I have caught glitches in our billing, amounting to well over $____ annually.
- Through my network, I have reached significantly more job seekers than my predecessors.

Be sure to show the results of your efforts:

- As a result, not one of our ____ has been late.
- After I started overseeing the proposals, we won 20 percent more work than this time last year.

- This allows me to _____, which is why I have been able to _____.
- We have a 25 percent higher recruitment and retention rate than before.

When You Get Turned Down for a Raise

Find out why. Learn what you can do. And come back again.

- What can I do to get a raise?
- Should I be focusing on any particular aspect of my performance to improve my value to the company?
- How can I become a better performer?
- What are the attributes you look for when determining whether to increase an employee's salary?

Part Eight

Relationship Quagmires

No kidding. You shouldn't have love affairs at work. You shouldn't watch sexy movies on the Web. And you shouldn't e-mail your beloved during company time. But face it, we're human, right? Actually, no. At work, we have to set certain aspects of our humanness aside, at least temporarily, so we can thrive as professionals. In fact, romance acts as putty sticking to our feet, keeping us in place, and, depending on the romance, creating a big mess.

But what happens when cupid slings his arrows in the workplace. What do you say to the coworkers who are smitten? And what about those altogether unwanted gestures from the guy who flirts at the copy machine or the unwanted candy and flowers your boss sent you? Ignoring these situations is foolish, unlikely, or even impossible. So here are a few pointers followed by perfect phrases you can't do without:

- *Measure the offense.* Romantic situations at work have various degrees of seriousness, and you should act according to the circumstances involved in each of them. If a person asks you out on a date and you say no, that's one thing. If he or she keeps pestering, that's more serious. If that person follows you home, sends you e-mails, or makes kissing sounds as you pass, that's harassment. Of course, employees who reveal their affections at the proverbial water cooler can be equally and unhealthily distracting. So determine the degree of the offense, and react in kind.
- *Report to the right source.* In some cases—possibly many cases—you may need to report the difficult situation to an authority. Only, pick your authority carefully. If you're a

woman and your boss is a man, he may not be responsive to your complaints that a male is pestering you. Similarly, if you tell a manager of either gender, he or she may not be aware of the steps you should take. Instead, you may need to consult with your HR Department or even an attorney before taking steps.

- *Be clear about the outcome you want.* What is the outcome you want? For the behavior to end? For the offensive couple to move to a different part of the building—or the planet? Or do think the employee deserves more serious forms of punishment, including a lawsuit? You may need clarity about what you're thinking or feeling to get a better perspective about what you want. So before you communicate with anyone, get a strong sense of your own intentions.

When Two Employees Are Having an Affair

Okay, so the employees are having a love affair. Or maybe it's a sordid affair. Who knows? And frankly, it's none of your business—or anyone else's. Except that they make it so obvious. You know the syrupy glances, the muffled conversations, and the inappropriate gestures in the parking lot. If this were high school, all right. But it isn't, and their interactions are distracting to everyone on your team. So they better cool it, and these perfect phrases will certainly help.

When Addressing One of the Amorous Employees

- If you and _____ are interested in each other in a nonprofessional way, please be more discreet.
- If you want to make so much noise chatting and laughing, you should wait until work ends. It's distracting to people.
- You and ___ need to keep your workplace relationship as professional as possible. If you want to go beyond those limitations, do so after hours.

When possible, mention the effect their behavior is having on other people in the office. This will ensure that they won't dismiss your complaint by calling you a "busybody," "uptight," or a "prude."

- Several people from the ___ department have complained about your behavior.
- Apparently you were carrying on when ___ brought a client into the office. We were all embarrassed.
- Because both of you were making jokes and insinuations throughout the meeting, people complained that they had a hard time focusing.

Be sure to rely on what other people said they felt—not on what you believe they felt:

- The consultants said they find the two of you "annoying."
- Our customer said he was "surprised" that people in our office carry on that way.
- People on my team were commenting on your relationship before the meeting started.

When Discussing That Behavior with Your Boss

- ___ and ____ have been touching each other in a nonprofessional manner. This poses problems in front of customers.
- We need to make sure that ___ and ____ either take separate lunch breaks or remember to return to the office on time.
- ___ and ___ have been having long conversations that involved lots of laughing. Several people from the ___ office complained to us about it.

Steer clear of judgmental language that might weaken your point:

- They're behavior is disgusting.
- Frankly, I think it's gross that they behave this way.
- They're being ridiculously immature.
- I think they're an embarrassment to the company.

When Interrupting Them in the Act

- Excuse me, but we are at work.
- You two have to cut this out. It's embarrassing to everyone.

- Go somewhere else if you feel amorous.
- Would you mind respecting the professionalism of our office?

When Explaining That Behavior to a Client or Someone Else Who Happens to Be Passing By

- Excuse them. I need to have a talk with them.
- We're actually a professional organization—they won't get away with behavior like that.
- Sorry you had to see that. They're both actually great employees, but their relationship seems to have gotten out of hand.
- They're being goofy. After you leave, I'll let their manager know, and I can assure you they'll stop.

Quick tip: When discussing romantic or otherwise nonprofessional interactions, better stick to formal language. In fact, the less description and the more general, the better. This is the antithesis of what you generally try to achieve in business writing. Here's a list of dos and don'ts phrases. Let your imagination do the rest.

Don't

- Dating each other
- Going out
- Having an affair
- Being erotic, sexual, or sensual

Do

- Acting inappropriately
- Having a nonprofessional relationship
- Touching each other
- Being together in a social context

When You Receive Inappropriate Overtures from a Boss

This situation is obviously problematic. You don't want the overtures and didn't ask for them in the first place. Even more, your boss has power over your raises, promotion potential, and, in many ways, your future. Obviously, you shouldn't yield. Nor should you decide you'll find another job. Why leave behind colleagues and work that you love? Instead, you should take control, get support if you need it, and continue moving ahead. These phrases will help support you.

When Confronting the Boss

At the Moment of the Advance

- Remember I'm an employee, and our relationship is and will remain professional.
- No, I won't be able to go out for dinner—I prefer to keep our relationship strictly professional.
- I never date anyone at work.
- I like to keep my private life separate.

In an E-Mail Later
This e-mail should also serve as documentation if your boss attempts to retaliate or doesn't change the behavior.

- In your office, you _____. This is not the first time you have done this; in our meeting last week you _____, and on Friday, as I was leaving after the meeting with my team, you ____. Please respect my professional boundaries.

- As I stated in your office earlier today, I am not interested in any type of nonprofessional relationship at work. I will not bring this subject up again and assume the same holds true for you.
- I found the comment that you made earlier today "_____" troubling. Please respect my professional boundaries.

If He or She Sends You a Gift

- I am returning the ____ that you left in my desk drawer this morning. Please recognize that as an employee, I cannot accept this type of gift.
- Although the ____ that you left at my desk were beautiful, we need to maintain a strictly professional relationship in every sense.
- The ____ that you left in my mailbox was quite a surprise, but my relationship with you must be clearly professional. Since ____ is perishable, and will only spoil if I give it back, I will leave it in the lunch room for everyone to share.

When Documenting the Event

It's critical that you document every interaction since the situation could come down to your boss's word against yours. Be clear about times, dates, and the gestures or words that passed between you. If anyone witnessed the event or has had similar experiences, be sure to document that, too.

Be Specific

- The morning of ____, the boss called me into his room. Then he proceeded to _____. I immediately told him his behavior was inappropriate and left the room. _____ saw me leaving and asked what was wrong. I didn't respond.

- On ___ at _____, the boss did the following: _____, _____, and _____. This was the second time this occurred. The first time was on _____. Both times I said that unprofessional behavior was wrong in the workplace, especially toward an employee.
- The boss sent me flowers with the words_____ on the card. I e-mailed him immediately after to restate that my relationship is professional. The card and e-mail are in my files.

Note: Be sure to leave a copy of your documentation at home, just in case the boss should rummage through your files to delete them.

Be clear and emotion-free—even when discussing your feelings.

Don't

- I was horrified and sickened by what he said.
- I think *she is disgusting.*
- After he said that, I wanted to take a shower.
- I think she is the most revolting person I know.

Do

- When I spoke, my voice was shaking.
- I left the room so quickly, ___ asked me what was wrong.
- I removed my hand from his immediately, took my notebook, and left the room.
- I was so surprised, I shouted.

Use Direct Quotes Where Possible

- When I entered his office, he said: "_____."
- After he did that, I said: "_____." He said: "_____"
  back to me.
- I told him then, and in my follow-up e-mail:
  "_____."

When Bringing the Issue to Your HR Department

E-mail HR that you want to establish a meeting, but make sure the confidential conversation is face-to-face. Here are some perfect phrases for discussing this difficult situation:

- I am having some problems with my boss. He has been making inappropriate advances . . .
- My boss has been harassing me recently. Although I tell her that I only want a professional relationship, the advances continue. For example, on . . .
- My boss has been ____, ____, and ____. For example, on ____ he . . . I have told him that I had no interest and sent several e-mails. These are in my file.

When a Coworker Comes On to You

When a coworker makes advances, you have more to lose than you think, so use the perfect phrases with care. Yes, you can tell your coworker to buzz off, but beware. He or she might spread rumors, pester or even harass you during the workday, or get hostile because you rebuffed him or her. Here are some ideas of what to do.

Be Clear and Unambiguous

The First Time a Situation Occurs

- I do not believe in workplace relationships, so please don't ask me again.
- You need to keep your hands to yourself.
- No, I'm sorry, but I am not interested in going out with you. I do not mix professional and personal relationships, especially with dates.

The Next Time a Situation Occurs

- Don't ever talk to me that way again. I demand respect, and if you don't give it, I will take action.
- Do not touch me anywhere or for any reason. This is inappropriate at work.
- As I said, I will not go out with you—during or after work—so please don't bring it up.

If the Situation Persists

- I told you on _____ and ___ that you should respect my boundaries and leave me alone. If you invade my space one more time, I will contact security.

- I am going to report you because you keep pursuing me although I have been clear that I am not interested.
- This is my last warning. You must stop making comments like that to me, or I will report you to security.

Quick tip: If you threaten a coworker, make sure you mean it. And yes, do follow up. If your coworker threatens you, even once, report this person immediately.

Document the Interactions

Like any situation where an employee or manager is giving you a hard time, be sure to document in clear and specific terms:

- On _____, _____ asked me if I would _____. When I said that kind of language was inappropriate, he laughed and repeated the comment later that day. My coworkers, ___ and _____, overheard the comment and will support me in this claim.
- _____ said that if I didn't drive home with her that night, she would tell people that "_____."
- Three times last week, on ___, ___, and ___, he made rude comments including _____.
- Although I told _____ to respect my space and my professional boundaries, she _____ twice last week, once on ___ and the other time on _____.

After an encounter, ask fellow coworkers if they overheard the interaction. If so, ask if they'd be witnesses if your boss, or someone in HR, asks.

Discuss the Situation with Your Boss

- I have been having trouble with _____, and you need to intervene for me.
- _____ has been harassing me in the office. I have two examples that occurred recently and can illustrate the problem_____.
- Recently, ___ has been approaching me on matters that are inappropriate for the office and, for that matter, outside of work. The first time this occurred . . .
- _____ recently said ___ and ___. I told him that I would talk to you unless he stopped.

Be sure to document the conversation with your boss. And remember, your boss is responsible for taking action in a case like this.

When a Client Bothers You or Your Employees through Lewd, Rude, or Other Inappropriate Behavior

That bothersome client is more than bothersome. He or she is harassing you or your employee. Yet that person also pays the bills and brings in a renewed source of profit. So what now? Do you tell the client to get lost? Or do you tiptoe your way around the poor behavior? The answer, as you'll see from these perfect phrases, is neither. You act in the clearest and most professional manner and hope that he or she respects that position.

When Warding Off Polite Overtures

- Thanks, but I don't think so.
- No, thank you—we have company policies that prohibit us from even discussing the issue at work.
- I appreciate the offer, but no.
- I'm sure it would be fun, but I better not.
- No, I'm sorry. I don't date people I know through work.

If you respond in writing to any overtures, blind "cc" your boss and/or someone in human resources. You never know—the client may get irritated and misrepresent your response or, worse, try to get you fired.

When Addressing Lewd or Forward Comments

- This is a workplace, and we must maintain a professional atmosphere.
- I don't appreciate those kinds of comments.

➥

- Comments like that are unacceptable at work. Please don't repeat them again.
- Please do not use language like that in front of me or my customers.
- Do not speak to me like that.
- I have no interest in hearing those kinds of comments. Please stop immediately.

When Insisting That a Client Stop Repeated Inappropriate Behavior

- You must stop saying things like that immediately, or we won't be able to let you in.
- This is a professional environment, and you must abide by our policies or we'll have to refuse you service.
- Do not come in again if you plan to say things like that again.
- When you say things like that, you are embarrassing our customers and humiliating our employees. You must stop at once.

When Telling the Client to Leave

When in the building, speak quietly yet clearly, so the client can hear you but no one else detects the problem. If you work for a large organization and have a security guard, tell that person to be alert. If not, contact the local police department, say that you might be having trouble, and ask if someone could come by to assist, if necessary. Remind security personnel that you don't want to upset your customers.

- I'm sorry, but you'll have to leave the building. If you don't, we'll call security.

- Please leave the building quietly and respectfully. I don't want to embarrass you or anyone else by having to call security.
- You need to leave our office. Your tone of voice is disruptive to everyone here.
- You must go right now. I have alerted the police, and they're on the way. So avoid embarrassing yourself or anyone else and leave now.

When Telling a Client by E-Mail Not to Return

- I'm sorry, but we must warn you that you are no longer allowed on our premises because of your behavior on ___, ____, and ____.
- Please note that we have alerted our security officer that you are no longer permitted in our building.
- As of ___, you are no longer allowed in our building because of the incidents on ___ and ___. If you need to finish any business, please e-mail ____, at_____.

Make sure that you do not insult or humiliate the client; keep the most professional tone possible.

Don't

- You are a despicable person.
- Everyone here hates the sight of you, so just don't come in again.
- We really resent all the disruptions you've caused.
- You're sick.
- You're pathetic.
- You have serious problems and need to see a shrink.

Do

- Your behavior has been upsetting our employees.

- Your comments are insulting. Although we told you to stop, you have persisted nonetheless.

- You have said these inappropriate comments loudly, upsetting our customers and our employees.

- These insults have created disruptions during the meeting. As a result, our consultants have been unable to move forward with the project.

When Responding to Indecent E-Mails

Don't respond—just make sure that person's e-mails head straight to your spam filter. But do alert security and let them know you don't want the customer on the premises again by forwarding an e-mail that says this:

- I have been receiving e-mails like this one from a customer. I don't want him on the premises again.

- Several of us have been receiving explicit e-mails from our customer. We're going to block her e-mails from getting through, but also need to ensure that she is not allowed in the building. What should we do?

- One of our customers has been sending e-mails like this one. The employees feel threatened and are concerned that he will come on the premises and embarrass us. What should we do?

- We need to stop the customer who sent this from entering our building.

When a Client's Employee Is Rude, Lewd, or Disruptive

When Arranging a Time to Talk through an E-Mail

- We have been having a problem with one of your employees and were hoping you can help.
- Could you please talk to one of your employees on our behalf?
- We need to talk to you about one of your employees.

Quick tip: When addressing the topic directly, make sure you know exactly what you want the client to do as a result. Talk to the employee so the behavior stops? Replace that employee with another one?

When You Want the Bad Behavior to Stop

- Your employee ____ has a history of ____. For example, on ____ he ____. Could you please discuss this behavior with him so it stops?
- Could you please tell your employee ____ to stop ____. Several of my coworkers have complained about this behavior and feel uncomfortable working with her as a result.

When You Want the Employee to Stop Coming to Your Office

- One of your employees, ____, has been ____ our employees. So we cannot let him into our office again.

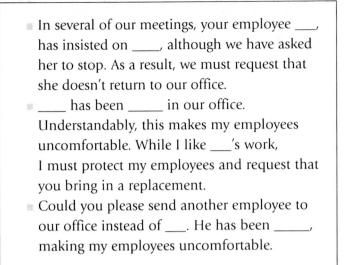

- In several of our meetings, your employee ___, has insisted on ____, although we have asked her to stop. As a result, we must request that she doesn't return to our office.
- ____ has been _____ in our office. Understandably, this makes my employees uncomfortable. While I like ___'s work, I must protect my employees and request that you bring in a replacement.
- Could you please send another employee to our office instead of ___. He has been _____, making my employees uncomfortable.

When an Employee Uses Inappropriate Materials or Accesses Adult Web Sites at Work

Hard to imagine, but more than half of online pornography is viewed in the workplace. What a person does outside of work is his or her business, of course, but inside the office, this poses unique problems. Obviously, the employee should be engaged in work, not adult viewing. As well, other employees or clients may catch sight of the material and feel uncomfortable or worse. So better not shrug and ignore the problem—but address it immediately.

When Confronting the Employee Directly

State how you know the employee views the material, so he or she can't say you're making false accusations. Then tell that person to stop. If necessary, tell him or her what you'll do next.

- I noticed some explicit images on your computer screen. This makes me and other people uncomfortable, and you should stop.
- Several employees have complained that they've seen explicit images on your computer screen. You must stop viewing this material in any form while at work.
- While repairing your computer, our technical assistant found that you have bookmarked explicit Web sites. As you know, this is inappropriate for the workplace. You must stop doing this, or I will have to take disciplinary measures.

When Notifying a Manager

- Several times this week, I've noticed explicit images on _____'s computer screen. Could you confront him or her on this matter?

- _____ watches explicit videos at work. I know this because_____. I do not feel it is my place to say anything and was hoping you'd take action.

- As my manager, I thought you should know that several of my coworkers and I have seen explicit images on _____'s computer screen.

- I thought you should know that _____views explicit images at work. While this makes me uncomfortable, I do not feel it's my position to say anything.

When You Are the Manager in a Large Company with Policies Dictating Behavior

While you must protect the employees who told you about the situation, be sure the person knows that others are aware of the situation, as well.

- Several employees have informed me that you have been viewing explicit material during work hours. Our policy states that this is unacceptable and grounds for dismissal. So take this as your first warning.

- I noticed that you are viewing explicit material on company time. According to policy _____, employees who engage in this behavior can be fired without a warning. Since you are an otherwise good employee, though, I am willing to give you another chance.

- Our company policy, under the Codes of Behavior section of our handbook, states that employees are not allowed to view explicit or other adult materials in the workplace. Several employees have notified me that you have been viewing these sorts of materials and e-mailing images around the office. If this occurs one more time, we will be forced to fire you.

> *Remember:* It's always best to e-mail this kind of message so you have a record. If you discuss it face-to-face, send an e-mail afterward, confirming your discussion.

When You Are the Manager in a Small Company without Policies Dictating Behavior

- I have just learned that you are viewing explicit material at work. This intimidates other employees and creates an uncomfortable work environment. You must stop at once, or I will be forced to fire you.
- I just learned that you have been viewing explicit behavior and have explicit materials at your desk. Because one of our employees spoke to you about this previously, and because this creates a difficult environment for us all, you must leave the office until I determine the next steps.
- Several employees have commented on your use of explicit materials at work. If I hear another complaint or see any indication, I will fire you. Be aware that your computer is company property and I can, and will, access it to make sure you have not repeated this behavior.

Acknowledgments

As always, lots of thanks to Donya Dickerson for asking me to write this second book of perfect phrases. It's been fun and cathartic. Who else can take difficult events and make them valuable to others? Also, I thank Grace Freedson, my agent and friend, for finding great projects like this one. Thanks go to all those folks who continue to make my life meaningful—Adam, for patiently waiting out the hours when I sat at this computer; Dan, for his everlasting support; and all those clients, friends, and associates who give me confidence, inspiration, and laughs. And, of course, thanks to those of you—you know who you are!—who conjure those difficult situations.

About the Author

Management and communications expert and talk radio host of *The Greater Voice*, Susan F. Benjamin reaches thousands of listeners throughout the world each week. Publications from the *Wall Street Journal* to the *Chicago Tribune* have featured Susan's novel approaches, while her columns about communications-related issues have appeared in newspapers including *USA Today*, the *Miami Herald*, the *Chicago Tribune*, the *New York Daily News*, and hundreds of others.

Susan's books include *Instant Marketing for Almost Free* (Source Books, 2007), *Quick and Painless Business Writing* (Career Press, 2006), *Perfect Phrases for Dealing with Difficult People* (McGraw-Hill, 2007), *Project Management for Top Performers* (Source Books, 2007), and *Manager's Answers* (Source Books, 2008), among others. Susan has discussed her books on CNN, National Public Radio, and other broadcasts. As a speaker, she regularly gives presentations for groups ranging from ASTD to Women Corporate Executives.

A former professor, Susan mentored academics at Harvard University and MIT. She participated in a White House initiative on Plain Language under the Clinton-Gore administration, trained over 100,000 employees in numerous venues, and has given keynote and other addresses. She has consulted for Liberty Mutual Insurance Group, Fleishman-Hillard International Communications, the National Geospacial-Intelligence Agency, the Federal Communications Commission, and many others.

Susan's research includes assessments of organizational processes and studies on how language affects employee responsiveness. Articles about these findings have appeared in publications such as *Scribes Legal Journal, Clarity, Government Executive*, and *Employment Management Today*.

Susan studied philosophy and writing at Boston University and Bennington College. She received her Master's in Writing from Lesley College, where she worked with C. Michael Curtis, senior editor of *The Atlantic*.

The Right Phrase for Every Situation…Every Time.

Perfect Phrases for Building Strong Teams
Perfect Phrases for Business Letters
Perfect Phrases for Business Proposals and Business Plans
Perfect Phrases for Business School Acceptance
Perfect Phrases for College Application Essays
Perfect Phrases for Cover Letters
Perfect Phrases for Customer Service
Perfect Phrases for Dealing with Difficult People
Perfect Phrases for Dealing with Difficult Situations at Work
Perfect Phrases for Documenting Employee Performance Problems
Perfect Phrases for Executive Presentations
Perfect Phrases for Landlords and Property Managers
Perfect Phrases for Law School Acceptance
Perfect Phrases for Lead Generation
Perfect Phrases for Managers and Supervisors
Perfect Phrases for Managing Your Small Business
Perfect Phrases for Medical School Acceptance
Perfect Phrases for Meetings
Perfect Phrases for Motivating and Rewarding Employees
Perfect Phrases for Negotiating Salary & Job Offers
Perfect Phrases for Perfect Hiring
Perfect Phrases for the Perfect Interview
Perfect Phrases for Performance Reviews
Perfect Phrases for Real Estate Agents & Brokers
Perfect Phrases for Resumes
Perfect Phrases for Sales and Marketing Copy
Perfect Phrases for the Sales Call
Perfect Phrases for Setting Performance Goals
Perfect Phrases for Small Business Owners
Perfect Phrases for the TOEFL Speaking and Writing Sections
Perfect Phrases for Writing Grant Proposals
Perfect Phrases in American Sign Language for Beginners
Perfect Phrases in French for Confident Travel
Perfect Phrases in German for Confident Travel
Perfect Phrases in Italian for Confident Travel
Perfect Phrases in Spanish for Confident Travel to Mexico
Perfect Phrases in Spanish for Construction
Perfect Phrases in Spanish for Gardening and Landscaping
Perfect Phrases in Spanish for Household Maintenance and Childcare
Perfect Phrases in Spanish for Restaurant and Hotel Industries

Visit mhprofessional.com/perfectphrases for a complete product listing.

Learn more. Do more.

THE IDEAL PERFORMANCE SUPPORT SOLUTION FOR MANAGERS AND SUPERVISORS

With over 30,000 phrases, *Perfect Phrases for Managers* is an unmatched digital resource that provides managers at every level with the skills they need to effectively manage any situation.

From performance reviews to documenting problems, to motivating and coaching teams, to managing difficult people and embarrassing situations, this performance support tool will help your company create an environment for exceptional performance.

Go to **www.perfectphrases.com** to learn more about *Perfect Phrases for Managers* and how you can access:

- A "Things to Consider" section with hundreds of bite-size coaching tips
- Audio clips from actual conversations
- Strategies for opening up healthy communication

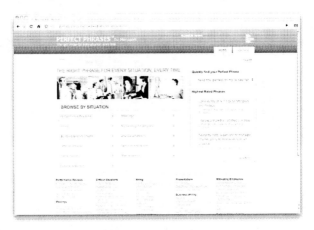

The right phrase for every situation, every time.

Visit www.perfectphrases.com to learn how your company can qualify for a trial subscription.

Learn more. Do more.
MHPROFESSIONAL.COM